On Sunday mornings I mix five simple ingredients into supple balls of dough, comforting harbingers of homemade pizza dinners for the week ahead. After a long work day, these silky rounds are quickly and easily stretched into crusts to be smeared, dotted, and draped with delicious toppings; the perfect meal in mere minutes. More than dinner, a homemade pizza is shorthand for happiness. It's reassurance that all the heaviness of the world can be held at bay—if only for a little while—by a combination of wholesome stuff, like bubbling mozzarella, sweet fennel sausage, and balsamic-glazed radicchio.

TRULY *Madly* PIZZA

TRULY *Madly* PIZZA

One Incredibly Easy Crust, Countless Inspired Combinations
& Other Tidbits to Make Pizza a Nightly Affair

SUZANNE LENZER

foreword by Mark Bittman

photographs by Christopher Testani

Rodale books may be purchased for business or promotional use or for special sales. For information, please write to: Special Markets Department, Rodale Inc., 733 Third Avenue, New York, NY 10017.

Printed in China

Rodale Inc. makes every effort to use acid-free ♾, recycled paper ♺.

Book design by Kara Plikaitis

Photographs by Christopher Testani

Prop stylist: Carla Gonzalez Hart

Library of Congress Cataloging-in-Publication Data is on file with the publisher.

ISBN-13: 978–1–62336–218–8 hardcover

Distributed to the trade by Macmillan

2 4 6 8 10 9 7 5 3 1   hardcover

RODALE

We inspire and enable people
to improve their lives and
the world around them.

rodalebooks.com

For my mom and dad, who together taught me to love cooking,
storytelling, and dinner.

And for Ken. Because without you, Bub,
none of it would matter.

CONTENTS

Foreword

I have watched Suzanne Lenzer grow as a home and professional cook. I even like to think I helped her. But when it comes to pizza, she's helped me: Her near-obsessional dedication to getting the crust just right was admirable; it took years, but she's done it. When I make pizza at home (which, admittedly, is not weekly, although that's admirable, too), I use Suzanne's crust—and, now that I think about it, the rest of her methods—and I'm repeatedly thankful.

In fact, I still call her for advice, but with the publication of *Truly Madly Pizza*, I guess I won't have that excuse any more. It's all here.

Suzanne's cooking philosophy and mine track closely: We both believe that cooking is a daily activity and one that need not be especially challenging or complicated. Pizza, of course, is a perfect example of that. When I first started cooking, no one—literally no one that I knew—made pizza. When my friends and I began baking bread, we realized that pizza was another possible avenue.

So I made decent pizza, for years. But, as with bread and just about anything else you cook, it's not all on the same level; there are better recipes and techniques and not-such-great ones. There is also skill development; that is, practice.

As I said, Suzanne tackled pizza with a vengeance. And, as is often the case with cooking discoveries, accidents and mistakes helped. Persistence helped, too, and I remember the day a few years ago when Suzanne arrived at a video shoot and said, "Wait 'til you try this crust." When I did, I was amazed: It had crunch, pull, toughness, tenderness, and flavor—it was the best pizza crust I'd ever had, and it was baked in a normal oven. (By me, for that matter!)

I'd say this about any cooking technique, but you can do this too; I've done it many times since then, without Suzanne making the crust for me. It's a slightly unorthodox method, but not weird or difficult in any way.

Which leaves toppings. Toppings are all about palate. Regardless of yours, you'll find toppings here that really appeal to you.

Perhaps more important, you'll find directions for taking those ingredients you love most and figuring out how to use them on custom-made pizzas (not as difficult as it might sound) that suit you perfectly. Suzanne's palate is broad and eclectic, and the suggestions here range from the classic to the adventurous, but they all sound delicious to me.

The package here is a stellar and simple dough recipe with easy-to-follow and smart techniques, along with perfect baking and topping instructions. It's all you need to make great pizza—every week.

—MARK BITTMAN

I believe in rituals. When I fly, I listen intently to the safety demonstration. I know that life rafts won't help me much if catastrophe strikes between New York and California. There is, as far as I know, no large body of water in the middle of Kansas. But it makes me feel better knowing that I've done what I can to respect the gods and ensure our safety at 30,000 feet. Some call this a superstition, but to me it's a ritual—one that gives me the sense that I have some control over forces that are, in truth, utterly out of my control.

That's what pizza nights do for me, too. They're a routine, a habit, a practice, a psychological talisman; a regular event that I cling to in order to feel that my life has some semblance of order—when often it doesn't.

No matter what the first day of a new week throws at me, no matter how looming the rest of the days before the weekend seem, pizza night promises me something familiar, something reliable, something known. Pizza night is more than dinner: It's confirmation that all the heaviness of the world will be held at bay—if only for a little while—by a combination of bubbling mozzarella, sweet fennel sausage, and balsamic-glazed radicchio.

This ritual came about out of pure laziness. I started making pizza crusts on Sunday mornings so that pulling dinner together during the week would be easier. Those early-morning dough fests have become known around our house as Sunday Pizza Factory. After the cats have been fed and the coffee is brewing, I whip up pizza dough for the week ahead—my kitchen counter becoming something of an assembly line covered with batches of rising dough.

Here's how it began: As he left on Monday morning, preparing himself to face the first day of the workweek, Ken would inevitably turn to me, offer up a kiss good-bye, and ask "Are we having pizza tonight?" until finally it was just part of our familial fabric, as expected as a "bless you" after someone sneezed. Mondays were our first official pizza night, but as I got more creative with toppings and playful with combinations, other nights of the week soon followed suit. Sometimes it was two, sometimes three, and I'm slightly embarrassed to admit that once we even succumbed to our cravings and achieved what Ken coined a "perfect game"—nine straight nights of different homemade pizzas. You have to love a guy who doesn't simply tolerate but actually encourages such batty culinary experiments.

Which brings me to one of the best parts of this pizza obsession: the community aspect of it all. I am the keeper of the crust, there's no doubt, but Ken is a willing participant when it comes to making the myriad toppings. It's a way to spend time together in the kitchen and hash out the events of the day while I stretch the dough and he slices. Okay, so ours is a very small community. Happily, one crust is the perfect size for two.

No, we're not a terribly social couple, but we have found that entertaining is a more engaging and collaborative activity when pizza is on the menu—everyone gets a say in what goes on top and has a hand in helping pull it all together. Which

is good for me in a personal growth kind of way because it forces me to relinquish my slightly structured (some might say controlling) side and let others help out. Pizza with friends compels me to loosen up, to worry less about presentation, and to succumb to the truth (which I happen to firmly believe) that dinner is about punctuating the day with a sip of wine, a story, and more often than not in our house, a slice.

The truth is, making pizza is fun. And children are especially smitten by the process. While spending a week with friends and their two little ones in Umbria a couple of summers ago, we were tickled to discover a wood-burning pizza oven on the premises—an amenity that made each day another excuse for pizza. Olivia and Joseph, ages 5 and 7, would clamber up on chairs to stand beside me at the counter in the morning and help make the dough; then each evening we'd take our same places, and they would happily tear at basil, tug at mozzarella, and decide what toppings would go onto what pie. They were both brazenly bossy and sweetly stubborn in how they kneaded the dough and chose their ingredients. Following my directions was short-lived, but again, making pizza became a remarkable lesson in letting go and embracing the process, no matter how messy or misshapen. There was something delightful about how proud they were producing pies of their own creation.

Suffice it to say, eating homemade pizza is never dull. The variety of flavors available when a ball of dough lays stretched out seductively upon a peel are endless. Admittedly it's taken years of modification to get the technique just right and the crust just so, but all the various iterations along the way have

held up their end of the bargain regardless of their outcome—even when they were too cake-y, too cracker-y, too thick, or too thin, every single crust has provided a sense of calm. No matter that they weren't always consistent, let alone perfect; a slice of a homemade pizza always reassures me that whatever the next day dishes out, it really won't be that bad.

The Crust (aka My Obsession)

Even with a gifted cook for a mom, growing up in Los Angeles meant that tacos, tamales, and taquitos were more standard dinner fare than pizza. When we craved pizza, there was Mazzarino's in Sherman Oaks—a red leather Italian place that we went to every now and then when we lived in the Hollywood Hills—which served up thin-crust, red sauce–smeared pepperoni and mushroom classics. At least that's how I remember it. Later, when I was 12 and we moved to the west side, there was Louise's, a small take-out place across from the Brentwood Mart that had two fascinating things going for it: handsome delivery boys and a great crust. When my parents went out with friends, Louise's was my sister's and my favorite dinner option, and while the boys who showed up with sturdy white pizza boxes in hand were undeniably part of the attraction, for me it was mostly about that crust.

Louise's crust was thin until it suddenly wasn't. Forming an inch-thick ring around the cheese and toppings was a chewy, char-dotted, hole-laden, flour-dusted crust that put all other pizza I'd tasted to shame. It wasn't heavy or doughy, just a hint tangy and toothsome. I loved this crust so much that as

I'm prone to do with other delicacies (crispy chicken skin comes to mind), I saved it for the "dessert" part of dinner, eating the triangle laden with toppings first and making my way with anticipation to that golden curve of bread last. Not one to stand on ceremony, I would also gladly (and still do) eat any and all discarded scraps of crust left on the plates of my dinner companions. A disgusting habit perhaps, but when it comes to a good crust I have no shame. So captivated was I by this crust that I went to bed on those take-out nights dreamily looking forward to breakfast leftovers; even cold, when the cheese had solidified to a near waxy consistency and the springy crumb turned tough, I happily tugged at it till my teeth ached.

Other pizzas, and in turn crusts, also crossed my radar. There was a birthday dinner at Spago (it was LA in the '80s and Wolfgang Puck was all the rage), and a pizza there delighted my taste buds, though I haven't the slightest recollection of what was on it. In my twenties, Ken and I found ourselves upstairs at Chez Panisse in Berkeley, and a nettle-topped beauty was placed before me. More than transformative, that pizza was transcendent. I can still see it if I close my eyes (thankfully this was pre-iPhone and tableside food photography wasn't ubiquitous yet; you actually had to remember transporting meals). But beyond these two "special occasion" pizzas, my experience with revelatory crusts wasn't very broad and my love for pizza wasn't all that encompassing. Certainly I liked a good slice, but it wasn't until I began making dinner regularly for a man who is passionate about his pie that I began to see the possibility pizza offered, the tabula rasa that a good crust delicately smeared, scattered, and dotted with thoughtfully chosen toppings could provide.

The first dough I can honestly remember making was from a small, square cookbook my parents gave me by Norman Kolpas, appropriately entitled, *Pizza California Style*. The crust was pretty traditional if I recall correctly, but it was the author's flair for combinations that captured my imagination. He had the gumption to put things like sun-dried tomatoes and duck on a pizza, the moxie to brazenly mingle caviar and crème fraîche (looking back, there is an abundance of crème fraîche on display in his pages). One plucky vegetarian option is called Asparagus Tips Alfredo, while another racy effort is Smoked Oysters with Provolone and Smoked Mozzarella—a virtual smoke-and-cheese-fest. Kolpas used goat cheese, Gouda, and Fontina long before anything but grated mozzarella was the norm; he gamely skipped the red sauce in favor of pesto. His avant-garde approach to pizza even inspired me to shape one unfortunate nouveau affair into a triangle (though in fairness, I'm not sure I can actually blame him for that misstep). Suffice it to say, it was with this slim 1989 volume that I became fascinated with making pizza and realized there were no limits to what a "pie" could be, as long as the base—the crust—was worth writing home about.

My Go-To, Tried-and-True, Know-by-Heart Pizza Dough

As someone addicted to baking bread—from the whole-grain-hippy-dippy-seed-laden bricks I labored over in college to the artisanal loaves inspired by Chad Robertson at San Francisco's famed Tartine Bakery that I now make—pizza crust is the perfect quick fix. It's an immediate gratification kind of bread making, one that satisfies my desire to feel the dough in my hands regularly in a low-maintenance, commitment-light kind of way. Pizza dough doesn't demand the time that other breads do, and while some recipes do require long rises (the all too common and totally unnecessary "until doubled in size" directive), my years of tinkering and tweaking have led me to the belief that a very short rise time is the secret to a great homemade crust.

My rather long journey to this discovery started with something one of my teachers in culinary school said about "retarding" the activity of yeast. He told us that by refrigerating dough, you could slow down the rise process and control the flavor and consistency of it more effectively. At the time, it didn't mean that much to me, but after reading a recipe for pizza dough by the chef Giorgio Locatelli, I started to believe that all the recipes asking cooks to get a good puffy rise out of dough for what is in essence a flatbread didn't make a lot of sense. In Locatelli's recipe, he calls for a short rise (20 minutes), then actually pulls the pizza out into its final shape before letting it chill for another 4 or so hours in the fridge. In essence, he gives the yeast a short window to come alive before slowing it down in its final flat form to help develop flavor.

I tried his approach with great success, but for someone who wants pizza to be easy, I needed to be able to freeze the dough, and I couldn't see doing that after having spread it into a 12-inch round (I also don't have the luxury of a fridge big enough to store said round of dough). So I bundled my crust up in plastic wrap and froze it—my hope being that as the crust thawed, the yeast would slowly come back to life and the flavor would develop, but that any breadiness would be held at bay. It worked. Freezing the dough in a ball and allowing the thaw to serve as an extended rise was perfect for a home cook like me who wants to be able to pull dinner together without much fuss (turns out it also works if you simply refrigerate the dough for a day or so). By tightly wrapping the dough in plastic and constraining its ability to expand, the more complex flavor blooms but the texture remains airy on the edges with a nice chew and very thin in the center. And the entire process takes less time and effort. Ta-da.

The one other really clever trick Locatelli taught me when I began dabbling with his *grissini* recipe is a quick fold-and-dimple of the dough before letting it rise, ostensibly to get more air into the crust. (Interestingly, Chad Robertson also uses a folding technique in his artisanal bread baking.) After you make the dough, you stretch it out into a longish rectangle, use your fingers to make dents or dimples all over it like a focaccia, and then fold it in thirds like a letter, continuing to poke it after each fold. Truthfully, sometimes as I do this I wonder if it's just silly—but like so many things in cooking, I believe it helps make the dough better, and two of the masters I trust seem to embrace aspects of the practice, so I keep doing it. It certainly doesn't hurt.

Of course, just as there are tons of recipes for pizza dough, there are also a million opinions on what makes a delicious crust. For me, a crust should be thin in the middle, thicker at the edge, and crisp with holes in it, like an artisanal rustic loaf. It should offer up a bit of chew, but never be bready or dense, and it should have a hint of char in places—ideally on the bubbles that arise around the edge and underneath. Most of all it should be light and have a slightly complex flavor to it, not floury or yeasty tasting. With my recipe, like all recipes, you'll find there's variation. Not just between yours and mine, but between yours on Monday night and then on Thursday night. Unlike a professional kitchen, the home kitchen is subject to constant variability—that's both the fun and the frustration of it. The temperature in your kitchen, how accurately you measure your ingredients, whether you leave your dough in the fridge to thaw, how long you leave it wrapped on the counter before stretching it, how long you let it sit on the peel before putting it in the oven, and of course, how hot (or not) your oven is. All of these things and more will contribute to each pie being slightly different, but that doesn't mean they won't all be delicious.

Some Good Things to Know in No Particular Order

If you're like me and you plan to make pizza night a once- or twice-a-week routine, or at least a frequent event, there are some things worth knowing that will make it easier on you and more enjoyable in general. Let me first say this: I love to cook. And I'm lucky enough to have found a way to make my living by cooking. As a food stylist and recipe developer, some days I come home from cooking all day and still want to make an inspired dinner. That's sort of nuts, and even I'm amazed by it. But then there are the other days—well, most of the other days really—when I come home and want a glass of wine and something soothing to eat, something that I can rely on to be delicious but also relatively healthy (more on this in a bit),

something that feels like what home cooking should be but doesn't require me to actually do a lot of cooking once I'm home. That's where pizza comes in.

With pizza—and specifically this pizza recipe—I can pull a lump of dough and a few bits and pieces from the freezer on my way out in the morning and know dinner will be taken care of. By the time I get home, the stuff in the fridge will be thawed, I'll pour a glass of wine, turn on the oven, and have a shower. I'll make a salad and stretch out a crust, scatter whatever I've foraged from the freezer, fridge, and cupboard over the top, and slide it into the oven. Dinner will be homemade, it will be made with real ingredients I've collected either at home or on the way home, it will be fun to eat and good for us, and rarely will it be the same thing twice.

Pizza Is Not Junk Food

So first, let's get the healthy thing out of the way. Pizza is not bad for you, and homemade pizza, I'd argue, is downright good for you. Unless you truly can't tolerate gluten, my pizza dough recipe is made from all wholesome ingredients that won't hurt you (and if you're someone on a gluten-free faddist tear, you shouldn't be reading this anyway; it will just make you envious). It's also made with a very specific amount of flour (i.e., if you're freaked out about carbs, this is the recipe for you). You'll know exactly how much you're eating every time because every crust is the same—in my world, one pizza provides two adults with a moderate-size meal. Unlike pasta where you can make the whole box and just keep going back for more, with this pizza you can't overeat unless you're willing to either overcook (meaning make more pizzas) or eat the whole thing yourself.

As for the cheese factor, again, if you use the amounts in the recipes (and you don't eat a bunch of other fattening stuff all day long or double the quantities here), these pizzas are probably better for you than most other things you're eating. The key to a delicious pizza is moderation—a little bit of a few wonderful ingredients is what you want so you can really enjoy the flavor combinations. These are not topping-laden, cheese-smothered, thick-crusted affairs. They're satisfying, satiating slices of good stuff.

The Freezer Is Your Pal

Most of the time I live in a New York City apartment. It's not the smallest apartment, but it's not that big either. My kitchen is actually probably only about 20 square feet (so okay, maybe it's on the smaller side), but I manage to make it work. One little secret: I don't have a full-size refrigerator or freezer. After about 12 years with a really terrible kitchen (I had a 20-inch stove and 8 inches of counter space), we decided it was time to renovate and I had a *Sophie's Choice* of sorts to make: proper-size stove or full-size fridge. Having cooked on that small appliance for many years and knowing I shop almost daily, I went for the stove and decided to live with my shoebox of a refrigerator. We did however shove a small freezer into one closet, and small or not, that freezer is one of my favorite kitchen tools, next to my knife and my food processor.

One of the most revealing discoveries in my pizza-making life came when a chef I was briefly assisting told me that mozzarella can be frozen with good results. I don't know why this surprised me so much, except that I assumed, like freezing milk, freezing would ruin the consistency of a fresh cheese. I was wrong; mozzarella freezes beautifully. Certainly I would always opt for fresh if life were perfect, but good, fresh mozzarella (the kind you buy in an Italian delicatessen floating around like so many white seals in an ocean of milky water) goes off so quickly that you spend all this money and often end up with most of it turning sour before you've used it. At least that's been my experience. Plus, you're melting it, meaning the consistency is going to change under exposure to heat anyway. What you're after is that sweet milky flavor, and the freezer helps preserve that. To me the trade-off of always having a small lump of good-quality stuff in the freezer is worth the wrath I'll hear from my cheese-making and cheese-mongering friends (I apologize in advance to you, Lou and Sal at Di Palo's, forgive me).

Then there's my other freezer staple: breadcrumbs. As a bread baker (and overall bread lover), I always keep a large bag of bread scraps in my freezer, along with a companion bag of breadcrumbs. Whenever a nub of bread is left over and just too stale to turn into toast, it gets tossed in the bread bag. Then, every so often (usually right after Sunday Pizza Factory while the food processor is still out and the counter is laden with rising dough), the collected bits of bread are blitzed up into crumbs, some akin to coarse sand or gravel and some left the size of large pebbles, the variation being exactly what I want when it comes to toasting them with a couple glugs of olive oil, a clove of smashed garlic, red pepper flakes, and

maybe some fresh oregano. Whether you want to invigorate a bowl of pasta, make a last-minute gratin or fruit crisp, or, as I'm prone to, add a bit of crunch to the top of pizza, keeping homemade breadcrumbs (from truly great bread, I should add) in your freezer at all times is a habit worth forming.

Beyond lumps of mozzarella and an absurdly large bag of breadcrumbs, at any given time in the bottom drawer of my freezer you will find countless pizza toppings that include but are not limited to: pancetta, bacon, roast chicken, meatballs, caramelized onions or leeks, ground sausage, broccoli rabe or broccolini, sautéed mushrooms, tomato sauce, pesto sauce, roasted garlic, and even chicken livers. Some of this will be uncooked, but for the most part, this drawer of snack-size zip-seal bags will contain small amounts of leftovers—remnants from various dinners, or toppings that I've made in larger quantities on the weekend so that making pizza after a long workday isn't a chore. These snack bags and salvaged yogurt containers may make me look like a crazy person hoarding unidentifiable scraps, but they provide us with an almost endless array of options for easy weeknight dinners.

The point is: Leftovers are a godsend to the pizza maker. That's why with many of the recipes in this collection, you'll be making more than you need for one pizza, especially when it comes to sauces or meat. It's actually easier to make a cup of pesto than a tablespoon or two. And there's simply no point in roasting a small piece of pork—it's just as much work to make a large piece, and you'll be endowed with dinner for many nights to come. Or, if you don't fancy roasting something just for pizza, add an extra pork chop to the pan one night. Then tuck that extra one away for later in the week.

Making chicken tenders for the kids? Toss a couple extra in the pan and stick them in the freezer for shredding later.

Some people love to cook, and a long day is no deterrent. If that's you and you feel like roasting a chicken, there's a foolproof recipe in the book (see Whole Roasted Chicken, page 213). Throw some potatoes in the pan beside the bird and let them cook in the glistening fat for a warming dinner tonight, then pick the bones clean and use those leftovers for a pizza tomorrow. The point is, leftovers of any kind—whether you set out to make them or find yourself facing a fridge full of bits and pieces—are a large part of the enjoyment of making pizza at home. Especially when you want to go beyond the recipes here and get creative on your own. So start saving things you might otherwise think are too negligible to bother with: that half an onion or last quarter bulb of fennel, those few grilled vegetables or slices of steak no one finished, the extra grated Parmesan that didn't get sprinkled on the pasta. It's all fodder for fabulous combinations.

A Food Processor Is Nice but Not Necessary

My crust recipe is easy for two reasons. One: It only rises for 20 minutes. Two: You can use a food processor. These two things make the entire process incredibly fast and clean. Usually it takes me almost as much time to pull the flour, yeast, olive oil, sea salt, and warm water together from their various places around the kitchen as it does for me to make the crust. Then it takes nearly as long to clean up as it does for the crust to rise. Which is why on Sunday mornings we make multiple batches—once everything is out, it's just as easy to make a bunch of crusts and toss them all in the freezer as it is to make just one recipe.

Certainly the food processor is essential to the ease factor in this recipe, but it's not crucial. In fact, you don't have to use a food processor at all. Like almost any dough or batter out there, you can make it by hand if you're either so inspired or lacking in the necessary tools. I have over the years managed to make a cheesecake in a blender (rather effectively, I might add), roll many a piecrust out with a wine bottle, and pipe French macaroons with a zip-seal plastic bag. When you need to make do, well, you do. Which is why it's worth mentioning that if you really want to try your hand at pizza crust, you shouldn't feel like you have to make an investment in a food processor immediately (though if you become a convert to the pizza-making way of life, you'll want to).

To make the crust by hand, what you need to know is that it'll be slightly messier (the flip side of that being you won't have to wash the food processor) and it will take longer, as you have to knead the dough the old-fashioned way. You will also have to use more flour during the kneading process to keep the dough, which is intentionally sticky, from sticking too much. This means it will have a slightly different texture when it's baked. If you'd rather make the dough by hand, the main recipe includes directions on how to adjust your technique.

Stones Are Great, but a Baking Sheet Will Do

For years I made my pizza (and all the various iterations it took to get to this exact pizza recipe) on a baking sheet (my

favorite baking sheet actually has crosshairs engraved across it from so many years of running the pizza cutter back and forth across it). Those pizzas were good, really good, but I kept reading in various cookbooks how much crispier they would be, how much better my crust would taste, and how much more toothsome the crumb would be if they were cooked on a blisteringly hot stone. Still I resisted. Why you may ask? The truth is, I was intimidated by the peel—the flat wooden paddle with a long handle one uses to transport the pizza to the stone. The notion of getting a flat round of sticky dough off a peel onto a stone inside an oven raging at 550°F just seemed like a really risky premise to someone like me (i.e., clumsy). It seemed like an accident waiting to happen, a feat of kitchen gymnastics I would almost certainly screw up. My feeling on the subject was pretty simple: Let's just not dabble in the inevitable. Let's keep the burned arms and ruined dinners to a minimum. So I happily used a sturdy baking sheet and made really good pizzas.

But then I went to culinary school and had to use a peel to prove my mettle in front of my pastry instructor. I would like to be able to say that it wasn't that terrifying—the truth is it *was* terrifying . . . but I did it. With a few starter motions to make sure the pie wasn't sticking to the thick layer of cornmeal I'd spread between it and the peel, I gained confidence (not a lot, but enough). Then, with a deliberate forward-moving shove into the blazing hot oven, the peel sliding just over the top of the stone, I tugged backward and recoiled from the oven with an empty peel. It was over in just seconds; my pizza was situated on the stone and beginning to blister and bubble as hoped. It took many more practice runs to feel secure in my skill set, but like anything, once you get the hang of the motion it's really not a big deal.

Ken is still hesitant about the peel. I regularly say, "Here, you put it in the oven," only to see him back up a step and say, "No way, I'm not doing it. You do it." But he *has* done it and if he'd do it more, he'd be fine. It's just a matter of using enough cornmeal to keep it from sticking, moving with conviction, and, I'm not ashamed to admit, a bit of preslide cheating: I'm sure it's sacrilege for professionals, but I'm not a pro, so I gently lift up the edges all around the pizza and check for any covert clinging. A few bad experiences when a pizza had sat too long in a warm kitchen and turned sticky have made me cautious. I admit I probably look like an amateur when it comes to the peeling off of a pizza, but I'm okay with that. There's nothing that breaks a home cook's pizza-making heart more than a pizza stuck halfway on the peel and halfway on the stone; it never ends well. Even though I've been making pizza now for a long time, I still play it safe, look a little silly, and shamelessly pray to the pizza gods every time. That's why if you wander unannounced into my kitchen at just the right moment, you may very well find me talking quietly to an unresponsive piece of dough, whispering sweet words of encouragement to my crust just before I give it that final, hopeful push into the heat.

Ingredients I Prefer

I'd love to say that any old flour and yeast combination will result in a perfect crust, but that hasn't been my experience. After years of switching between brands, playing with regular flour, bread flour, wheat flour combinations, and even Italian "00" flour, I've decided that King Arthur's Bread Flour is the most reliable. I've had brilliant successes with "oo" in wood-burning pizza ovens, but in my home kitchen I find that King Arthur is the way to go. I don't know enough about flour to tell you why this is my favorite, but I know it's wholesome, tastes good, and works. Period.

I have also had varied results with different brands of yeast. For years I used Fleischmann's Active Dry Yeast—the yellow and red packets that come in a perforated trio—and it worked fine. But then my mother-in-law started giving me packages of Dr. Oetker brand yeast. Not only would she stuff my stocking with these shiny green pouches at Christmastime, but I'd find them hidden in my slippers each time we went to visit her. Marguerite swore Oetker's was better than Fleischmann's, and with a constantly replenished supply, I quickly became a loyal user. She passed away very suddenly on Christmas weekend a few years ago, and I can't lie, to this day I try to stick with Oetker's as a way to keep her alive in my kitchen. Probably goofy, but there you go. In a pinch I also use Hodgson Mill Active Dry Yeast and have found it to be a good substitute when Oetker's isn't available. It may also be obvious to anyone who bakes, but you do not want to use fast-rising or rapid-rise yeast—you want active dry yeast for my recipe.

As to olive oil, this is completely a matter of personal preference, and there are a lot of conflicting opinions out there as far as I can tell. I know cooks who will only use extra-virgin olive oil for finishing and would never consider cooking with it (they say it turns bitter, though that's not been my experience). Other cooks I've talked to swear by Italian olive oil, others are adamant that Greek is the best, and some will only use Spanish. I've also been told that color doesn't matter when it comes to great olive oil and then had an Italian (who makes his own) tell me that color is a sign of depth of flavor. So who knows? I am devoted to California olive oil and, more specifically, to California Olive Ranch brand. A couple of years ago, I read an article by the inspiring *New York Times* writer Julia Moskin in which she evaluated various olive oils, and I was intrigued to learn that many imported oils are blends. California Ranch is not. It's also a great value (I go through a lot of olive oil, so for me cost is also a factor as well as flavor): A big bottle costs about $18 as opposed to upward of $30 for some imported brands. To my palate the California Ranch oil is lovely; it's subtle with just a whisper of verdant, earthy olive flavor and a hint of pepper, but not so much that you experience that throat-catching sensation (though I'm told that is also something some people strive for in an olive oil). For cooking, and especially for pizza making, it's hands down my favorite.

Salt. That's another complicated story. Most chefs I know swear by kosher salt, and for many years I did, too. That is until I met Mark Bitterman (not to be confused with my friend and mentor, Mark Bittman). Bitterman owns a small shop in my neighborhood called The Meadow where he sells salts from all over the world. He's an energetic, passionate man who is truly evangelical about all things salt. I could write a book about his philosophy on salt (though he already has, so that would be silly), but suffice it to say he changed my cooking life when he told me that kosher salt is basically a processed food, an industrialized ingredient coveted by chefs for its uniformity, not its purity. Tasting a variety of pure sea salts with Mark one day, I was riveted. Sea salt, what I'd always reserved for finishing, was what I should be cooking with. How could I have been so misguided?

Mark's argument for quality sea salt is compelling, but the moment of conversion took place for me when he said: "If you're willing to spend the money to buy a free-range, organic chicken, why would you season it with something that's highly processed and part of the industrial food complex?" I wouldn't. I mean I had, but now I would stop. Since meeting Mark I've tried to help spread his message, and the easiest way to do that is through having people taste the difference. Sea salt tastes like the sea; it's oceanic and briny and wonderful. Kosher salt is, well, salty. Chefs love kosher salt because its homogenous size will perform consistently from line cook to line cook. And it's cheap. But that's not what I'm looking for when I cook—I want my food at home to be pure and wholesome. Bring me my Maldon sea salt (flaky and full of salinity) or a nice fine sea salt that's alive with minerality any day. I'll save the kosher salt for scrubbing my cast-iron pans.

And here's a final thought on ingredients. When it comes to toppings, try to use good ones. You're going to a certain amount of effort to make your own crust, so don't skimp at the end. It's like buying an expensive dress and wearing cheap shoes. If you're going to the trouble, make it worthwhile. You're not going to layer a pound of meat on a pizza anyway, so buy the best you can rationalize. Fresh mozzarella (made by hand) is worth seeking out, but again, if you're at the market and all they have is a soft ball of mozzarella with a sell-by date on it, go for it. It's still better than buying a bag of preshredded, processed cheese. Whether you shop at a local farmers' market or a suburban grocery store, just try to buy the freshest, healthiest, most sustainable meat and cheese you can and you'll be fine.

Lastly, produce is simply better when it's in season, and it's usually more affordable. Buying stuff out of season means it's flown in from somewhere far away and you're paying for that flight. You'll likely find that the flavor suffers on those long-haul journeys, too. Instead, stay seasonal and get creative. When I lament not being able to make a certain apricot tart or fig crostata because the fruit isn't in season, Ken always jokes that "chocolate is always in season." And he's right (but it also means he'd rather I make something with chocolate than either apricots or figs). The same goes for canned tomatoes. There's no excuse for an anemic tomato on a pizza when you can buy a can of San Marzanos, squeeze the seeds and juice out, and chop them up. There's also no crime in buying a bag of frozen peas or opting for chard over tender greens if that's what looks best and it happens to be mid-March. Recipes are only as useful as they are relevant, and if you're trying to make a summer pizza in the dead of winter, you'll be disappointed. I'm guilty of this, too—getting attached to an idea of what dinner might be only to admit that I'm off by a few months. But this is how I discover new combinations—buying what's ripe, what's in season, and what is the closest to wholesome and pure as possible.

Don't Forget the Wine

Part of pizza night for me is the ceremony of the meal as well as the sustenance of the food. Which is why it would be negligent of me to not make mention of wine. To my mind, wine is as much a part of dinner as the food being served, and while I'm not a connoisseur by any stretch, I do know what I like.

We have what we call "house wines" or "pizza wines," those bottles we buy by the case, usually French, Californian, and New World Sauvignon Blancs, Spanish Albariños, and Italian varieties from Orvieto and Alto Adige. They're the ones we know we like and can buy confidently and quickly—wines that are reliably good and affordable (and that I can pull out of the wine fridge without risk of opening something fancy by accident). Sure it's fun to spend an hour or so in the wine shop browsing for new and exciting bottles to try, but having some familiar favorites is like having a broken-in, faded pair of jeans—they fit well and are comfy to slip into after a long day.

Then there are the more indulgent wines we covet to savor with friends or on weekends when time slows down a bit. For me these tend toward slightly more extravagant French Burgundy and Loire-style whites—Pouilly-Fumé, Pouilly-Fuissé, Sancerre, and Chablis—dry whites that are perfect with almost any pizza as they're crisp and lively, but not as oaky as their California cousins whose fuller, more buttery flavor (and higher alcohol content) I tend to find a little overpowering. Ken loves his spicy Zinfandels and gutsy Cabernet Sauvignons, but generally the reds we drink with pizza lean toward the lighter. A satiny Pinot Noir is frequently our mutual preference no matter what the topping or season may be. There's also something festive about opening a bottle of rosé on the first nice spring-summer evening. I may not be staring out at the Mediterranean or a vineyard in Provence, but with a glass of blush-toned wine in hand and a gentle breeze overhead, it's fun to pretend. The point is I don't buy into the high-minded wine-food pairings thing. I think the wine you choose to serve with your pizzas should be whatever you like—even if that's beer.

A Few Last Thoughts Before Dinner

I have a thing about pizza for sure, but even more, I have a thing about dinner; I believe in it like some people believe in going to church on Sunday. It's just something that, if you do it, you should do properly. You should cook, or at least prepare something, and sit down and eat it. And if you're with someone else, you should talk a bit, too. It's the way the day is punctuated; just as coffee or tea in the morning is preparation for what lies ahead, to me dinner brackets the day with a sense of closure, a time to chew through the day's events and to regain any lost equilibrium. It's the time to settle and regroup before whatever it is that you do each day starts all over again. And it's a time to eat something real.

That's not to say I haven't enjoyed my share of cold Chinese leftovers standing next to the sink or grazing over cheese and crackers after a big lunch, but these dalliances are definitely the exception—lost meals that almost always leave me feeling

slightly guilty afterward, as though I've knowingly passed a friend on the street without saying hello.

Just as some people are religious about their morning run or their weekly manicure, I am an acolyte, a devoted subscriber to the rite known as dinnertime. I believe it should entail something substantial, something that takes at least a little effort (dialing the phone counts once in a while, but pushing buttons on a microwave really doesn't). Yes, it's about food and sustenance, but perhaps more importantly, it's about nourishment: replenishing some of the emotional nutrients lost and scattered throughout the day.

This book is primarily one really useful pizza dough recipe followed by a lot of varied ways to keep your pizzas interesting. But I find that part of any inspired meal goes beyond the main dish; it's the entire experience that makes a dinner special, from the snacks you have beforehand to the salad you serve, from the wine you sip to the company you share it with.

That's why in these pages you'll also find a selection of some of my favorite snacks—little bites designed to accompany a glass of wine while the pizza cooks, but that could just as easily make up a casual lunch for friends. There's also a smattering of salad recipes that I think accompany pizza really perfectly, ideas that you can take and adapt or adjust to suit your own taste and your own style of cooking. And then there are a handful of recipes that are meant to be cooked in advance and provide toppings for pizza, but that can also be dinner in their own right. Finally, there are a couple of stragglers, recipes that bear no direct relation to pizza, but that I mention along the way and just seemed too good to leave out.

MY GO-TO, TRIED-AND-TRUE, KNOW-BY-HEART PIZZA DOUGH RECIPE

Makes two 10- to 12-inch crusts | Serves 4

There are literally thousands of recipes for pizza dough out there, and while the ingredients are almost always the same—flour, yeast, olive oil, water, and salt—it's the proportion of these ingredients to one another and the way they are treated that leads to such variations in texture and taste. This recipe is the result of years of testing and tweaking, and what makes it so special for the home cook is that not only is the active time very short (less than 10 minutes followed by 20 minutes unattended), but the result is reliable. A stint in the freezer or fridge is part of what helps develop the flavor here, so making several batches at once and keeping them on hand is the way to go.

You'll notice in the recipe I give weight measures for the flour as well as an approximation in cups. This is because weighing ingredients in baking is essential for accuracy and consistency. My recipe was originally developed using 390 grams of flour, but here's the thing: I wanted it to be easier. So one day after measuring my ingredients out, I grabbed a set of measuring cups and translated the weight into cups. That day it was 2¾ cups. So that's what I began working with. But I've also tested my accuracy the other way—by measuring out 2¾ cups and then weighing it—and it's nearly always off by 10 to 20 grams. It's just the nature of working with flour: Sometimes it's finer, sometimes it's packed down more, it just varies. All that said, I generally use my measuring cups because it's easier and I have a pretty good sense of what the dough should look like when it's done. So I can wing it a bit and add a few drops more water if needed or a tablespoon more flour if the proportions are slightly off that day. In the beginning this will take some confidence, but once you get used to what the dough should look and feel like—very soft, a hint sticky, and just manageable—then you'll be able to gauge if you need a bit more flour or water without using a scale. The goal of this recipe is to be as simple and consistent as possible. If you prefer measuring cups, then use them; however, if you have a scale, it's certainly a more pristine way to go.

390 grams bread flour (about 2¾ cups)
¼ ounce active dry yeast (about 2½ teaspoons)
2 teaspoons sea salt
¼ cup extra virgin olive oil
1 cup warm water
2 to 3 tablespoons medium or coarse cornmeal

Food processor method:

In a food processor fitted with the metal S-blade, combine the flour, yeast, and salt and turn the machine on. Add the oil through the feed tube, then add the water in a slow, steady stream. By adding the water slowly, you can watch the dough come together and you'll get a sense of whether you should add more or whether it's too wet—it should look pliable and smooth after a minute or so of processing. (The more water you can add and still be able to handle the dough without it sticking to your hands, the better it will be.) Continue to process the dough for about 2 minutes. The dough should form a ball and ride around in the processor. If it does become too wet, add another tablespoon or two of flour until it's moist to the touch but can be handled easily. When the dough is done, it should be soft, slightly sticky, and elastic. It may also be hot from the machine, so be cautious.

Lay a piece of plastic wrap about 12 inches long on a clean work surface. Use your hands to press the dough into a rectangle on the plastic, about 8 inches long and 6 inches wide. Press your fingers into the top of the dough all over it, making indentations as though it were a focaccia. Fold the left third of the dough over and repeat the finger indentions on this folded section. Fold the right third over (as you would a letter) and use your fingers to make the indentations again. Cover the folded dough with plastic wrap and let rise for 20 minutes.

Hand method:

Combine the flour, yeast, and salt in a large bowl and mix. Add the oil and mix. Add the water slowly, mixing to create a dough. It will be sticky, especially at first. Flour a clean work surface, move the dough to the surface, and begin to knead it. Don't tear it, just push it back and forth and over itself again and again. Keep kneading it until it's soft as a baby's bottom—seriously, that is the best description of what your dough should feel like. As you're kneading it, moisture will rise to the surface and it will get stickier at times; use a bit of flour to keep it soft and pliable, but don't go overboard (as for the food processor method, the more hydration the dough can tolerate and you can handle, the better it will be). At this point, pick up the directions in the second paragraph for the food processor method (at left).

After 20 minutes, cut the dough in half and form each piece into a neat ball (each ball will make a 10- to 12-inch-round pizza). You can use the dough right away, but you'll find the texture of the crust will be a bit breadier and the flavor less complex (that said, I've done it many times in a pinch without complaint from anyone but the overly critical cook, i.e., me). Instead, for best results, I recommend freezing, which retards the yeast's activity—allowing for the flavor to continue and develop in the dough as it thaws, without letting it rise and become bready. (A similar outcome can be achieved by refrigerating the dough for up to 1 day, but if it's very warm or humid, even in the fridge your dough can expand relatively dramatically. I've had some break through the plastic on a warm July day even in the fridge. If this happens, simply unwrap, roll it back up into a ball, and rewrap. It'll be fine.)

To freeze and thaw:

After dividing the dough into 2 balls, wrap each ball tightly in plastic wrap and freeze immediately after wrapping. The morning of the day you plan to make pizza, take it out of the freezer and put it in the fridge to slowly thaw. Twenty to thirty minutes before making the pizza, pull the dough out of the fridge and let it come to room temperature while you prepare the toppings.

Shaping the crust:

Working with the dough in your hands (not flat on a work surface), gently begin to stretch the dough into a circular shape, pressing your fist into the center of the dough and pulling at the edges with your other hand. With both hands, stretch the dough, being careful not to tear it. Working in a circular motion, pull the thicker edges of the dough outward, letting gravity help you.

Continue to stretch the dough until it's relatively even in thickness (the edges will be thicker—that's okay) and you have the size you want.

To cook the pizza:

Preheat the oven to 550°F. (If I have time, I do this up to 1 hour before cooking so the oven is really hot.)

If using a stone and a peel:

If using a stone, put it in the oven to preheat, too. Dust the peel generously with the cornmeal. Follow the directions above to shape the crust, and when the dough is the size desired, carefully lay it on the peel.

If using a baking sheet:

Brush a large baking sheet with extra virgin olive oil and sprinkle it with the cornmeal. Follow the directions above to shape the crust, being careful to work it into the shape of your pan.

Top the pizza as desired and either slide it off the peel and onto your heated stone or place the baking sheet directly into the oven. Bake the pizza until the crust is golden and the cheese is bubbling, 6 to 10 minutes.

While I do have an outdoor pizza oven, all but five of the pizzas pictured in these pages were baked in my home oven at 550°F. During the photo shoot, we used my kitchen oven both to illustrate the point of this book—that you don't need anything special to make good pizza—and so we didn't have to worry about stoking a fire for five days straight. We did however use the wood-burning oven on our final day. Happily, I don't think you can really tell the difference between those baked in a conventional oven and those outside.

Variation: Whole Wheat Pizza Dough

I was very fortunate to have a fabulous mother-in-law. I know people complain about their in-laws, but I was tremendously spoiled to have Ken's mom, Marguerite, as mine. Like any relationship, it took some time to find our way, but when she died very unexpectedly a few years ago, I found myself mourning not just for Ken's loss, but for mine, too. Our friendship was of course a result of my being married to her son, but at a certain point that didn't really matter anymore; we were friends, plain and simple.

Ken and I cooked a lot with Marguerite, and while she wasn't an adventurous cook, she was an enthusiastic one. At some point she decided she wanted to make pizza, so we taught her, and while she claimed to use my recipe, I know for a fact she tinkered with it. She was adamant that a whole wheat pizza was better for you than all white flour pizza, so she started substituting some wheat flour for some white, slowly at first, but eventually her balls of dough were nutty brown in contrast to my corn silk–colored ones.

All that is a prelude to why a whole wheat crust variation is in this book. The weekend she passed away, at Christmas as luck would have it, we found ourselves thrown into a fog that's hard to explain if you haven't been through it. It all happened very fast, and in retrospect it's a blur of driving and sitting and hoping and driving and sleeping and sitting and driving some more. At some point, we left the hospital to go to her house to feed her cat, Coco (now our cat, for those who are curious). While we were there, I moved the crown roast that was planned for

Christmas dinner into the freezer so it wouldn't go off. That's when I noticed one of her pizza crusts nestled between the ice tray and the English muffins.

The crust I found in the freezer that day was the last one she made, and it was indeed, at least partly whole wheat. The day she died we came home, sat by the fire, made some phone calls, and watched as a blizzard moved in and blanketed us in snow. We also defrosted that lump of dough. That night I made a pizza with whatever I had in the house (I honestly don't remember now what it was) using that crust. It just seemed like the right way to punctuate a really awful weekend—with a really lovely pizza she had made, I like to think, just for us.

I don't usually make whole wheat pizzas—I like the taste and texture of all bread flour much better. But I know a lot of people want to add more whole grains into their cooking and out of respect for that, and affection for Marguerite, I can't help but share a whole wheat version here.

Everything is EXACTLY the same, just substitute half whole wheat or white whole wheat flour (King Arthur makes both, and Marguerite swore by the white whole wheat) for half of the bread flour. I've found this is the most the recipe can handle without becoming too dense and a bit sour tasting. If you want to play with less whole wheat flour that's fine, too—either way you'll get a nice crust albeit different in flavor and texture than one made with solely bread flour.

SAUCES, SPREADS, *and* SMEARS

As insistent as I may be about the importance of great crust on a pizza, I'm nearly as adamant about the right sauce, spread, or smear on said crust. The thin layer of flavor that lies between the crust and the toppings needs to be additive yet subtle, it needs to enhance the flavors of the toppings without overwhelming them, and it has to maintain the integrity of the crust—meaning not allow it to become soggy.

Many people (my dear husband included) feel that a pizza needs tomato sauce to be a *real pizza*. I beg to differ (and happily I've convinced him to expand his horizons as well). Tomato sauce is a traditional and admittedly lovely way to add flavor to a pizza and to tie all the various ingredients together. But there are many other options, especially if you don't plan to make your own tomato sauce (which I hope we can agree now is really the only kind you want to be using).

Here's a trick: If you don't have time to make a proper tomato sauce, brush your crust with a thin layer of good olive oil and spread thinly sliced Roma tomatoes or squeezed and roughly chopped San Marzanos (yes, from a can) over the top—this will give you both the moisture and tomato-y flavor you want. It may be simpler and less nuanced than a cooked and fully seasoned sauce, but it will still be delicious.

Even though I don't feel the need for tomato on every pizza, I do want some whisper of flavor between the crust and all else. Often I just brush my pizzas with a golden swath of olive oil to add a layer of fatty flavor. But when I'm making a pizza with bacon or pancetta, I opt to use the leftover fat rendered from the pork. I hear the gasps, can almost see the looks of horror that are staring back at this page right now, aghast at the idea of using bacon fat that way, brushing it liberally on a crust like so much butter on a piece of toast. But let me explain: This is truly one of the great delights of pizza eating—pork fat is the most incredible "sauce" you can use. It's just a bit smoky and slightly meaty, more of a fragrance than an actual flavor. It's subtle and substantial at the same time. Happily, it's also the easiest sauce to conjure up, being simply a by-product of a topping you're making anyway. Perhaps not as decadent as duck fat (coveted for fried potatoes), but those few tablespoons of porcine essence will provide you with a saucier pizza than you may ever have imagined.

Another one of my favorite ways to add flavor to a pizza instead of tomato sauce is with caramelized onions, leeks, or roasted garlic. All of these provide incredibly rich, earthy notes in the form of a "spread" or "smear." You can make them in large amounts and keep them frozen to use whenever, or if you find yourself with half a sweet Vidalia or red onion in the fridge, cook it down quickly for a last-minute pie.

Pesto—or "paste" in Italian—is another pizza smear I adore. The classic, made from basil, is a no-brainer, but I won't buy the packaged stuff even in a pinch. If basil isn't in season and I don't have any pesto in the freezer, I'd just as soon blitz up blanched broccoli rabe or kale, a handful of walnuts with some olive oil, garlic, and Parmesan for a nutty version, or throw a small bunch of tarragon, chervil, and parsley together for a more herbaceous twist. Honestly, if you're in a sauceless situation, there is always something better than store-bought bottles of tomato sauce or packaged pesto. When in doubt, olive oil (or bacon fat) can be a pizza maker's best pal.

ESSENTIAL POMODORO SAUCE *(for Pizza and Life)*

Makes about 1 quart

Looking at the ingredients and seeing how easy this sauce is, you wouldn't think it could be a life-altering addition to your cooking repertoire, but it is. And here's why: It's so simple, so pure, and so essentially what a good tomato sauce should be that life is just better when you have some in your freezer. But before I wax on too far I must confess, I regularly muck about with this recipe with wild abandon; it's just the way I cook. Yes, ideally a can of imported San Marzano tomatoes is what you want to use, especially if you're a purist. I'm more of an enthusiast, especially when it comes to using up what's sitting around. I regularly find myself with a half pint of grape or cherry tomatoes wrinkled and puckered and about to go off, a couple of larger tomatoes gone mushy too fast, or some Romas looking listless and anemic—none of which I can bear to toss in the compost. So I dice up the half red onion or shallot left over from something I can't recall, chop up the mix of tomatoes in their various states of impending decay, and I make an abridged version of this classic sauce. It's always slightly different and mildly haphazard depending on what I've got on hand, but it never seems to disappoint.

2 tablespoons extra virgin olive oil
1 small onion or shallot, chopped
3 garlic cloves, peeled and smashed
1 can (28 ounces) San Marzano tomatoes
Sea salt and freshly ground pepper
¼ teaspoon red pepper flakes (or to taste)
1 to 2 tablespoons sugar (optional)

In a large saucepan, heat the oil over medium-high heat. Add the onion and garlic, reduce the heat to medium, and cook, stirring occasionally, until the onion is tender and translucent and the garlic is very aromatic, 6 to 8 minutes.

Add the tomatoes (and their juices) and continue to cook, using a wooden spoon to gently break up the tomatoes. Season well with salt and pepper and add the pepper flakes. Cook for 12 to 15 minutes for the sauce to thicken a bit and so the flavors begin to meld. Taste and decide if you need to add more salt to bring out the flavor of the tomatoes or even a bit of sugar (this depends on the tomatoes and varies with every can).

Use an immersion blender (or a food processor or standing blender) to puree the tomato sauce. Taste again and season if needed.

REPERTOIRE-WORTHY PESTO

Makes about 1 cup

In cooking, there are shortcuts and then there is cheating. Canned beans and tomatoes are highly respectable short-cuts. Ditto for those plastic clamshells with prewashed baby arugula. Sometimes they're just in better shape (and easier) than a limp bunch tied with a rubber band. And I believe a bag of frozen peas can be a godsend. But there are some foods where cheating should never be excused—their pack-aged selves just aren't as good. Pesto is definitely one (and since we're on the topic, so is salsa). It's ridiculously easy to make, and even easier in larger quantities than small; I usually make a full batch and freeze most of it in tiny containers so there's always some on hand. To me, pesto is one of those sauces that even people who aren't really passionate about cooking should have in their repertoire. I'm not even convinced making pesto should count as "cooking" as all you need are fresh ingredients and a food processor. It's a lovely alternative to tomato sauce on pizza and, as a side note, it's also the fastest way to make a dazzling pasta dinner redolent of midsummer when you're stuck in deepest January.

1 large bunch fresh basil, leaves picked (about 4 loosely packed cups)
½ cup pine nuts or walnuts
1 garlic clove, peeled and smashed
¼ cup extra virgin olive oil, plus more as needed
½ cup freshly grated Parmesan cheese
Sea salt and freshly ground pepper

In a food processor, combine the basil, nuts, and garlic. With the machine running, add the oil slowly through the feed tube until the mixture is pureed. Add the Parmesan and pulse to combine. If the mixture is too thick, add another tablespoon or so of oil until you have the consistency you want. Taste and season with salt and pepper as needed.

You'll have lots leftover for multiple pizzas, so transfer the remainder to small airtight containers (some people use an ice cube tray and then put the frozen cubes of pesto into a resealable plastic freezer bag), drizzle a bit more olive oil over the top to prevent discoloration, and freeze. As a side note, I've heard the kitchen lore that you shouldn't freeze pesto once the cheese is incorporated as the taste will change, but I've never found this to be true.

CARAMELIZED ONION JAM

Makes about 1¹/₂ cups

I have a very good, very fast, very unorthodox way of making caramelized onions or leeks. It's one of my favorite parlor tricks and a cheat for sure; a part sauté, part braise method that takes half the time of proper caramelization but that tastes just as good on a pizza as the real deal—and means you don't have to spend more time making your toppings than you do your entire dinner. I'm sure some will frown on my unconventional approach, but it works for me. Traditionally caramelizing onions to that deep, nutty point means starting with a dry pan, lid on, and letting the heat from below and steam from within do a long, slow, weepy, wonderful thing. However, I find I can get a pretty close approximation of the same flavor and texture by simply browning the onions quickly and then adding water to braise them. The browned bits stuck to the bottom of the pan offer up loads of that earthy flavor, and instead of 45 minutes or even an hour of cooking, these are done in about 20 minutes. Use the same technique for leeks or red onions; if you want the flavor a little more intense, you can always sprinkle a bit of sugar over them at the end to sweeten and add some extra browning.

¹/₄ cup extra virgin olive oil, plus more as needed
4 large sweet onions (such as Vidalia) or red onions or 2 to 3 leeks (cleaned, white part only), very thinly sliced
Sea salt and freshly ground pepper
About ¹/₂ cup water

In a medium saucepan, heat the oil over medium-high heat. When the oil is hot, add the onions and sprinkle with salt and pepper. Reduce the heat to medium and cook, stirring frequently, until the onions begin to color, about 10 minutes. If the pan seems dry, add a few extra tablespoons of oil.

When the onions are golden brown on the edges or are beginning to stick to the pan, add the water. Stir and continue to cook until the liquid evaporates and the onions are very tender and have melded together in a tangle, another 10 to 15 minutes. Save any leftovers in small containers and freeze.

ROASTED GARLIC SAUCE, SPREAD, SMEAR,
or *What-Have-You*

Ken has a thing about raw garlic. Whether it's on pizza or rubbed on toasted bread for bruschetta, he complains that the untamed flavor of raw garlic sticks around way too long, like an '80s pop song you can't get out of your head (remember "Come on Eileen"?). So, in an effort to appease him, I've found that replacing raw garlic with roasted garlic is a dreamy solution. Frankly, roasted garlic tastes better anyway—it takes on a luscious nuttiness, and that overpowering, breath-of-fire flavor is almost totally muted. It's also one of those very rewarding cooking chores that require very little effort yet yield enough flavor to last a month or more. Roast an entire head of garlic and you'll use just a clove or two smeared on a pizza. The rest can be stored in small containers and frozen.

8 heads garlic
¼ cup extra virgin olive oil
Sea salt

Preheat the oven to 400°F.

Use a chef's knife to slice off the top third of the heads of garlic. Transfer the garlic heads to a baking sheet. Drizzle the oil over the garlic heads so it penetrates down into the cloves and sprinkle with a bit of salt.

Roast until the garlic is very soft, beginning to brown, and the cloves are starting to pop out of their skins, about 45 minutes.

When the garlic is cool enough to handle, squeeze the cloves out of their skins and into a single airtight container or multiple small containers so you can freeze it in usable portions.

PRESERVED LEMONS

Makes about 1 quart

I don't imagine I'm the only one who still gets care packages from her mom and dad, but instead of favorite baked goods, the boxes that my doorman hands me are full of limes. Not just any limes mind you, but Mexican limes. These thin-skinned, yellow globes are sweeter than a conventional lime and less acidic than a lemon, and they come all the way from my parents' garden in Los Angeles. Yes, it's a rather embarrassing truth that while I carry reusable bags to the market and have replaced all my lightbulbs with those curvy energy-saving ones, I have no qualms about having my parents send 10-pound boxes of citrus across the country by jet plane. It goes against all my ecoconscious instincts; but honestly, these are really good limes. So good in fact, that over the years I've wondered how I could make them last longer. Then my friend Elana gave me a recipe for pre-served lemons, that staple of Moroccan cooking that makes almost anything taste better. I use my parents' limes when I can, but any thin-skinned lemon will do (organic tend to be better simply because the skins aren't a half inch thick and mostly pith). Chopped on a salad, layered on a sandwich, scooped straight from the jar as a guilty pleasure, these lem-ons will brighten up almost anything—especially a pizza.

12 small, thin-skinned lemons (or Mexican limes, if you have them)
6 shallots, minced
6 garlic cloves, minced
5 tablespoons sea salt
6 tablespoons sugar

In a saucepan of boiling water, blanch the lemons for about a minute. Drain, rinse, and wipe them with a paper towel to get any wax off of them. Slice the lemons as thinly as you can, getting rid of any seeds and reserving the end pieces.

In a small bowl, combine the shallots and garlic. In a second small bowl, mix the salt and sugar. Using an airtight jar, make a layer of lemon slices on the bottom. Top this with a bit of the shallot-garlic mixture, then a good sprinkling of the salt-sugar mixture. Continue layering the lemon slices and the two mixtures, until the jar is almost full but not overly packed (the juices need some room to circulate). When you've filled the jar, press down on the layers gently to release some of their juice. Then, squeeze all the juice from all the reserved ends of the lemons into the jar. Seal tightly and shake the jar a few times.

Refrigerate the jar for 3 to 5 days to let the flavors fully meld, giving it a shake or two each day. Kept sealed in the refrigerator, they should last up to a month.

Use the slices whole or roughly chop.

SPICY CHILE OIL

Makes about 1 cup

*When I make my go-to Essential Pomodoro Sauce (page 25)
for pasta, I add red pepper flakes to give it some complexity.
However, recently I got a little heavy-handed with the red
pepper flakes. Okay, a lot heavy-handed. In an effort to
save the sauce, I did some research and found that, like
cream, butter will smooth out heat. In this case I didn't
want to make a cream sauce, so I added a good amount of
butter, softened the spice, and was rewarded with a volup-
tuous, almost silky, still-red tomato sauce. It wasn't what I
was aiming for, but dinner was salvaged (and I learned
something nifty about how spice and fat work together).
Every now and then, though, I have the opposite problem:
In trying to add heat to food so it has time to ease into all
the ingredients and round itself out, I go too light and I miss
that chile warmth on my tongue. When that happens and I
need to add a little boost of flavor, I turn to this über-easy
oil. It's like a happy afterthought.*

1 cup extra virgin olive oil
1 teaspoon red pepper flakes (or to taste)
4 to 6 dried red chiles

In a small saucepan, combine the oil, pepper flakes, and whole dried chiles.
Heat the oil over medium-low heat until just warm, about 5 minutes.
Remove the pan from the heat and let cool completely. When the oil is
cool, transfer everything (including the chiles) to an airtight bottle or jar.
Refrigerate the oil for up to 1 month.

WALNUT PESTO

Nuts seem to provoke strong sentiments in people. What kinds they like, what foods they belong in, and often, most emphatically, what foods they most definitely do not belong in. I have my own issues with nuts. Not eating them, but burning them. I've been cooking for the better part of 30 years, and I still manage to routinely burn walnuts, pine nuts, pecans, you name it. And yes, I've tried setting a timer. That's the beauty of this recipe for me: You don't bother to toast the nuts. The buttery, earthy, richness of the sauce comes from the raw flavor of the walnuts combined with the garlic and cheese. A quick blitz in the food processor and you're rewarded with a pizza smear, a pasta sauce, a crostini topping . . . whatever your heart desires. And no risk of char.

1 cup walnuts
1 tablespoon Roasted Garlic Smear (page 29) or 2 garlic cloves, peeled and smashed
About ¼ cup extra virgin olive oil
½ cup finely grated Parmesan cheese
Sea salt and freshly ground pepper

In a food processor, combine the walnuts and roasted garlic and blitz until finely ground. With the machine running, add the oil through the feed tube until the walnuts turn into a thick but relatively smooth paste, a minute or so. Add the Parmesan, season with salt and pepper, and puree again. If the mixture is too thick but tastes rich, add a tablespoon or so of water to thin it. If it needs more body, add a bit more oil. Transfer to an airtight container.

FRUIT *and* VEGETABLE PIZZAS

My sister has been a vegetarian since she was 16. Ali was always a picky eater, and her early fussiness evolved into a passionate dedication to not consuming animals. I'm pretty sure it didn't help that as a nutrition major in college, she had to take a meat butchery class. I respect her commitment to vegetarianism immensely, and as an animal lover I've dallied with the idea of giving up meat at various points over the years as well. Honestly though, I've never had the guts to do it—and even if I did, I doubt I'd be very good at it. I enjoy meat, and I'm not great at all-or-nothing propositions. I'd rather accept my fate as a light meat eater than live as a struggling vegetarian, one who proudly lays claim to the label in mixed company and then falls off the wagon when it's just us carnivores and the chicken liver pâté comes out. I could see that happening, and it makes me cringe.

Label or not, Ken and I do eat a predominantly vegetarian-esque diet in our house. Breakfast is an established routine of homemade granola and fruit. Weekday lunches for me are often a hunk of cheese and a few crackers, half an avocado, or, if I'm on set, a salad. And dinner, well, dinner is often pizza—and very often pizza topped with little more than a tumble of vegetables and a tangle of cheese.

Here's the thing: I don't consciously think "Tonight I'm going to make a pizza with just vegetables on it." I think, "It's Tuesday. What do I have? A zucchini and some fresh ricotta in the fridge. I'll pick up some tarragon on the way home. We're set." Or just as often, I'm at the market roaming idly for inspiration when I spy a lovely Japanese eggplant. En route to scooping up this slinky aubergine, some shiitake mushrooms might catch my eye, along with a small bundle of fuzzy oregano. Again, dinner is decided—and the notion of meat never entered the picture.

It sounds random, and I suppose to a degree it is, but ingredients that go together in one preparation play well in others as well, especially on a crust; it's the perfect place for mixing and matching vegetables. Think of it as a lab or a workspace. What's the worst that can happen if I layer cannellini beans with cherry tomatoes and some baby spinach? How far awry can I go tossing broccoli florets with red onion slivers, red pepper flakes, and Parmesan? Not very. It's low-risk playing around with vegetables, and it usually leads to good things.

Today I have a standing repertoire of vegetable pizzas (I don't call them vegetarian for fear of alienating omnivores like my husband) that I go back to again and again, and while some require barely more than a vegetable peeler to pull together, others are a bit more time-intensive. Some are classic combinations that will be familiar and comforting, but others are more inspired; variations on vegetable dishes I've eaten and loved and feel deserve their own spot on a crust. Some are the result of meanderings through the farmers' market, times when a particular parsnip or pear seems to beckon from afar. And many are just happy accidents, unexpected combinations that came about as I stared hopefully into the fruit bowl or the fridge, desperate to wrangle up a meal at the end of a long day.

Note: All pizzas serve 2.

LEEK, POTATO, TALEGGIO, AND FRESH THYME

There was a time when I would have questioned putting a potato on a pizza—two starches felt like overkill. But then a few years ago, my mom told me about a pizza she'd had with potatoes, fresh rosemary, and Parmesan, and I couldn't get the idea out of my head. Little did I realize I was a very late adopter of a classic combination. The key is making sure the potatoes are sliced paper-thin so they stay tender on the inside and slightly crisp around the edges. Layer these gossamer spuds over buttery leeks, add some creamy Taleggio, and finish it off with fresh thyme and grated Parmesan, and trust me—the skeptic—there's nothing lovelier.

2 tablespoons extra virgin olive oil
1 large leek (white part only), cleaned and thinly sliced
Sea salt
¼ cup water
1 medium Russet potato, sliced paper thin (ideally with a mandoline)
1 ball pizza dough (page 16), thawed if frozen
About 3 ounces Taleggio cheese
Leaves from 3 to 4 sprigs fresh thyme
Freshly grated Parmesan cheese

Preheat the oven to 550°F.

In a medium skillet, heat the oil over medium-high heat until it shimmers. Add the leeks and sprinkle with salt. Reduce the heat to medium-low and cook, stirring frequently, until the leeks begin to soften, 10 to 12 minutes. Add the water to the pan to keep them from browning and help them braise. Continue to cook, stirring occasionally, until they meld together, another 8 to 10 minutes. They should have an almost jam-like consistency. (I usually have enough for at least 2 pizzas and just freeze the leftovers.)

continued

continued

Meanwhile, bring a medium saucepan of salted water to a boil. Add the potato and cook until the water just returns to a boil—the slices should be tender but not thoroughly cooked through. Drain and set aside to cool. (If your slices are really, truly paper-thin, you can skip this step and use them raw, but they do need to be almost sheer.)

Shape the pizza crust as directed in the master recipe. Spread the leeks evenly on the pizza crust using the back of a spoon, leaving about a 1-inch border all around and being careful not to tear the dough. Dot the leeks with walnut-size pieces of Taleggio. Place the potato slices on the crust in a single layer with the slices partially overlapping. Sprinkle the pie with the fresh thyme and some Parmesan.

Transfer the pizza to the oven and bake until the crust is nicely browned, the edges of the potatoes have colored and begun to curl, and the cheese is melted, 6 to 10 minutes.

Layer these gossamer spuds over buttery leeks, add some creamy Taleggio, and finish it off with fresh thyme and grated Parmesan, and trust me—the skeptic—there's nothing lovelier.

RAMPS WITH POACHED EGGS AND PECORINO

I had never heard of ramps, a kind of wild onion, until one spring about 15 years ago when I stumbled on them at the Union Square farmers' market in Manhattan. Smitten with their fluttery leaves and graceful cranberry-colored stems, I bought a bunch. Returning the next week, I was told that ramp season—late April to early June—was over. They were there, and then just as quickly they were gone. Like so many romances, I had fallen fast and hard, only to be left dumbfounded and distraught that our time together ended so soon. Five weeks? Six at best? So this was what "seasonal" meant. Years later I still remember sautéing that first bunch of ramps. It was an unusually hot spring evening, and Ken stood beside me as we experimented with these wild allium on my 20-inch stove—staring into the pan as their scallion-like heads turned pearly white in the olive oil, their crimped waists blushed deep burgundy, and their citron tails filled with hot air and puffed up, only to deflate and wilt into a wonderful buttery tangle. My love for ramps has endured all these years, and though their appearance in my life is regular, it's also fleeting. When they show up, I treat them as well and as diversely as I can. Somehow draping them over a pizza and bestowing a beautifully poached egg on them feels fitting for a transient and vagabond vegetable such as this.

1 ball pizza dough (page 16), thawed if frozen
2 tablespoons extra virgin olive oil
1 bunch ramps, trimmed but whole
Sea salt
About 3 ounces fresh mozzarella cheese, torn into bite-size pieces
About 2 ounces pecorino cheese, finely grated
1 teaspoon fresh lemon juice or any white vinegar
2 large eggs

Preheat the oven to 550°F.

In a large skillet, heat the oil over medium-high heat. When the oil is hot, reduce the heat to medium, add the ramps, season with salt to taste, and cook, turning frequently, until the bulbs are tender and the leaves have wilted and are just beginning to color, 4 to 6 minutes. Remove from the heat.

Shape the pizza crust as directed in the master recipe. Scatter the mozzarella over the pizza crust. Place the sautéed ramps evenly over the mozzarella and top with the pecorino.

Transfer the pizza to the oven and bake until the crust is browned and the cheese is bubbling, 6 to 10 minutes.

Meanwhile, bring a medium saucepan of water to a gentle simmer and add the lemon juice or vinegar. Crack an egg into a small dish or ramekin and gently pour the egg into the barely simmering water. Repeat with the remaining egg. Cook the eggs, keeping the water at a gentle simmer, until the whites have just set but the yolk is still loose, 3 to 4 minutes.

To serve, use a slotted spoon to scoop the eggs out of the water, dab the spoon on a paper towel as you remove each egg to drain any excess water, and place the eggs on top of the finished pizza.

Their scallion-like heads turned pearly white in the olive oil, their crimped waists blushed deep burgundy, and their citron tails filled with hot air and puffed up, only to deflate and wilt into a wonderful buttery tangle.

A TRIO OF TOMATOES WITH PESTO AND BURRATA

So here's the deal with this pizza: You can only make it for a few weeks each year when tomatoes are truly, honestly, purely perfect. You can of course try to make it at other times, but it won't be the same. The little yellow tomatoes need to be so sweet you almost want to save them for dessert, the Green Zebra tomato has to be firm and bright and citrusy, and the red heirloom needs to be red through and through and almost weep when you slice it. The pesto should be homemade, and the burrata, which means "buttered" in Italian I'm told, has to have a calming effect on all of these vibrant flavors. I know, this really does sound like the worst of foodie nonsense, but I promise, your taste buds will let a bit of snobbery slide on this one.

1 ball pizza dough (page 16), thawed if frozen
¼ cup Repertoire-Worthy Pesto (page 26)
1 medium red heirloom tomato, thinly sliced
1 medium Green Zebra tomato or a green heirloom, thinly sliced
A good handful of Sun Sugar yellow cherry tomatoes, halved
1 medium ball burrata
Sea salt and freshly ground pepper

Preheat the oven to 550°F.

Shape the pizza crust as directed in the master recipe. Smear the pesto over the surface of the dough using the back of a spoon, leaving about a 1-inch border all around. Lay slices of the two larger tomatoes evenly over the pesto. Scatter the yellow cherry tomato halves over the larger slices.

Transfer the pizza to the oven and bake until the crust is golden brown and the tomatoes have begun to soften if not blister a bit, 6 to 10 minutes. One minute before the pizza is done, slide it out from the oven and add a scoop of the burrata in each quarter of the pie. Return the pizza to the oven to let the burrata barely melt. To serve, sprinkle with salt and pepper.

SWEET AND SOUR ONIONS WITH BUTTERNUT SQUASH AND RICOTTA *(aka My Purloined Pizza)*

This recipe is hot. As in stolen. Or at least, so delicately adapted as to almost be a crime. I first tasted this combination of ingredients on a bruschetta made by chef Jean-Georges Vongerichten. In the version he shared with me (or rather, shared with Mark Bittman as I stood by, a very lucky sidekick), he fried thick slices of rustic bread in olive oil, then mashed roasted kabocha squash together with sweet-but-tart onions to spread on the toasts. To finish, he added dollops of fresh ricotta and vibrant mint leaves, creating a revelatory blend of sweet, tangy, creamy, and bright in every bite. Captivated by the complex flavors and stunning colors, I've taken the liberty of blatantly borrowing this idea. Admittedly this is a purloined pizza, but as any recipe thief knows, some things are just irresistible.

2 cups peeled and cubed butternut or kabocha squash
4 tablespoons extra virgin olive oil
½ teaspoon red pepper flakes (or more to taste)
Sea salt
½ large sweet onion, thinly sliced
2 tablespoons apple cider vinegar
2 tablespoons maple syrup
1 ball pizza dough (page 16), thawed if frozen
About ¼ cup whole-milk ricotta cheese
Leaves from 2 sprigs fresh mint, roughly chopped

Preheat the oven to 400°F.

On a baking sheet, toss together the squash, 2 tablespoons of the oil, the pepper flakes, and a sprinkle of salt. Roast, stirring every few minutes, until tender and slightly colored, 20 to 30 minutes. Remove from the oven and increase the heat to 550°F.

Meanwhile, in a medium skillet, heat the remaining 2 tablespoons oil over medium-high heat. Add the onion slices and sprinkle with salt. Cook, stirring frequently, until the onions are very soft and beginning to caramelize, about 15 minutes. Stir in the vinegar and syrup and reduce until the onions are the consistency of a loose jam, another 15 minutes.

Shape the pizza crust as directed in the master recipe. Using a fork, smash the squash until broken down but still fluffy. Smear the crust with the onion mixture, leaving about a 1-inch border all around, and top with forkfuls of the squash and dollops of the ricotta.

Transfer the pizza to the oven and bake until the crust is browned and the cheese has softened, 6 to 10 minutes. To serve, sprinkle the pizza with the fresh mint.

Admittedly this is a purloined pizza, but as any recipe thief knows, some things are just irresistible.

SHIITAKE MUSHROOMS WITH ROASTED GARLIC, THYME, AND TALEGGIO

The thing about pizza is it's really a blank canvas for anything delicious. Which is why I frequently borrow combinations of ingredients from other dishes I've made and just drop them on a crust. This is a mix of flavors and a technique that I originally discovered in a risotto recipe (thank you, Jamie Oliver). The technique for roasting mushrooms infuses them with an intense aromatic flavor while also caramelizing them perfectly—they don't get soupy—and the rich and earthy texture is the ideal foil to a warm, luscious (and yes, slightly stinky) Taleggio.

3 tablespoons extra virgin olive oil

2 cups sliced shiitake mushroom caps

4 to 6 garlic cloves, peeled and smashed

Sea salt and freshly ground pepper

4 or 5 sprigs fresh thyme, plus a few leaves for garnish

1 ball pizza dough (page 16), thawed if frozen

About 3 ounces Taleggio cheese

Preheat the oven to 400°F.

In a small Dutch oven or other ovenproof pan with a lid, heat 2 tablespoons of the oil over medium-high heat. When the oil is hot, add the mushrooms and garlic and sauté until the mushrooms just begin to soften, about 3 minutes. Sprinkle with salt and pepper. Add the thyme, cover, and transfer to the oven to roast until the mushrooms are cooked through and the garlic is very soft and fragrant, 6 to 8 minutes. Remove and set aside. Leave the oven on and increase the temperature to 550°F.

Meanwhile, shape the pizza crust as directed in the master recipe. Brush the crust with the remaining 1 tablespoon oil and dot with the Taleggio.

Remove and discard the thyme stems from the mushroom mixture, leaving behind as many leaves as possible. Scatter the mushroom and garlic mixture over the crust evenly.

Transfer the pizza to the oven and bake until the crust is browned and the cheese has melted, 6 to 10 minutes. Garnish with a few more thyme leaves.

PESTO WITH SUN-DRIED TOMATOES AND TOASTED PINE NUTS

Reading Eleanor Perényi's delightful gardening book Green Thoughts *a couple of years ago, I discovered that seeds bought in Italy are apparently far better than those we can get here in the States. Acknowledging the illegality of it, I was inspired on a trip to Rome to buy some basil seeds from a vendor in a market just off the Piazza Navona. Slipping them into my carry-on bag (along with a small glass bottle of premixed Campari and soda—Ken claims it was multiple bottles, but that's neither here nor there), I made it home with my smuggled seeds. They got off to a slow start in our shady back garden, but eventually, by July, they produced the most vibrant, delicate, abundant crop of basil imaginable. Whipped up into that classic Northern Italian delight pesto, paired with tangy, toothsome sun-dried tomatoes, and the crunch of a random pine nut, this pizza is like the classic Margarita on steroids.*

¼ cup pine nuts
1 ball pizza dough (page 16), thawed if frozen
¼ cup Repertoire-Worthy Pesto (page 26)
About 3 ounces fresh mozzarella cheese, torn into bite-size pieces
About 8 sun-dried tomatoes in olive oil, sliced

Preheat the oven to 400°F.

Spread the pine nuts on a baking sheet and toast until just golden, 4 to 6 minutes. Remove afrom the oven and increase the temperature to 550°F.

Shape the pizza crust as directed in the master recipe. Using the back of a spoon, smear the pesto lightly and evenly over the top of the crust, leaving about a 1-inch border all around. Scatter the mozzarella on the pie along with the sun-dried tomatoes. Sprinkle the toasted pine nuts on top.

Transfer the pizza to the oven and bake until the crust is browned and the cheese has melted, 6 to 10 minutes.

EGGPLANT, ZUCCHINI, ROMA TOMATO, AND CAPERS

My favorite way to make this pizza is by grilling the eggplant and zucchini. You can certainly sauté them—or, as my mom is prone to, just toss them on raw with a last-minute drizzle of olive oil. But the grilling adds an extra layer of flavor, a whisper of char that is really wonderful. This pizza is also an open invitation for improvisation if you have leftover grilled vegetables of any kind—fennel, endive, radicchio, leeks. Pretty much anything you threw on the grill the night before and tossed into a baggie as a leftover will happily work as an add-on or sub here. And a note about peeling eggplants: I don't. I like the toothsome outer skin and think it adds flavor and texture. Ken disagrees. So we compromise and I run a vegetable peeler down the eggplant, leaving half the strips of skin in place and half the flesh exposed. You end up with long stripes of bruise-colored skin against the creamy interior, and everyone ends up happy.

1 small eggplant, preferably Japanese or Italian, cut crosswise into ¼-inch slices
1 small zucchini, cut crosswise into ¼-inch slices
2 tablespoons extra virgin olive oil
Sea salt and freshly ground pepper
1 ball pizza dough (page 16), thawed if frozen
1 Roma tomato, thinly sliced
About 3 ounces fresh mozzarella cheese, torn into bite-size pieces
Leaves from 2 to 3 sprigs basil (torn if large) or fresh oregano
1 tablespoon capers, drained (or more to taste)

Preheat the oven to 550°F. Heat a grill or grill pan to high.

Brush the sliced eggplant and zucchini with the oil and sprinkle with salt and pepper. Working in batches if necessary, add the vegetables to the hot grill and cook until they release easily and are nicely charred on both sides, 6 to 8 minutes total. Remove from the grill.

Shape the pizza crust as directed in the master recipe. Top with the sliced tomato and mozzarella. Evenly distribute the grilled eggplant and zucchini on top of the cheese and tomato, scatter the fresh herbs evenly, and sprinkle with the capers.

Transfer the pizza to the oven and bake until the crust is browned and the cheese has melted, 6 to 10 minutes.

SUMMER SQUASH WITH LEMON ZEST AND RICOTTA

Zucchini and summer squash are vegetables that I seem to buy too much of when they're in season. I think what happens is this: I'm at the farmers' market, I want to capture summer in my bag, and I forget that I'm not running a small restaurant and we're not a family of eight. So into the bag go four goosenecked, lemon-yellow summer squash—then the chatty farmer with the bristle-brush white mustache tosses in a couple of zucchini for free because he's had a bumper crop. Now I have a lot of squash, and while they look beautiful in my vegetable bowl, they demand to be eaten or threaten to join the compost bin. So that's how this very simple summer pizza came to be. Drizzled with some lemon juice, a good grating of zest, and generous scoops of milky ricotta, the squash goes from too much of a good thing to, simply, a very good thing.

2 tablespoons extra virgin olive oil

2 small yellow summer squash, zucchini, or a combination, cut lengthwise into ¼-inch slices

About 1 teaspoon fresh lemon juice plus grated zest of 1 lemon

Sea salt and freshly ground pepper

1 ball pizza dough (page 16), thawed if frozen

¼ cup Caramelized Onion Jam (page 27)

About ¼ cup whole-milk ricotta cheese

Preheat the oven to 550°F.

In a medium skillet, heat the oil over medium-high heat. When the oil is hot, add the squash and cook until tender but not browning, 4 to 6 minutes. Add a teaspoon or so of lemon juice to the pan, increase the heat to high, and cook until the liquid has evaporated. Add the lemon zest, toss to combine, and remove from the heat. Taste and season with salt and pepper.

Shape the pizza crust as directed in the master recipe. Evenly spread the onion jam over the top of the dough, leaving about a 1-inch border all around. Lay the sautéed squash across the jam and finish with dollops of the ricotta.

Transfer the pizza to the oven and bake until the crust is browned and the cheese has melted, 6 to 10 minutes.

MIXED MUSHROOMS WITH LEEK JAM AND GRUYÈRE

Leeks are one of my favorite and Mother Nature's most versatile and scrumptious vegetables. Whether you sauté, grill, roast, or braise them, they just always seem to be there with a buttery, silky, almost sweet disposition. In this recipe, as in many of my pizza recipes, I use onions and leeks in place of a true sauce. By cooking them down to an almost jam-like consistency, they add a thin layer of flavor between the crust and other toppings, one you don't so much notice in texture as you do in taste. Adding the uninhibited earthiness of mixed mushrooms and an Alpine cheese like Gruyère to this pizza makes for a delicate and soothing tribute to autumn.

4 tablespoons extra virgin olive oil
1 large leek (white part only), cleaned and thinly sliced
Sea salt and freshly ground pepper
¼ cup water
2 cups sliced mixed mushrooms (cremini, shiitake, button, or other)
1 ball pizza dough (page 16), thawed if frozen
½ cup freshly grated Gruyère cheese
Leaves from 3 to 4 sprigs fresh thyme

Preheat the oven to 550°F.

In a medium saucepan, heat 2 tablespoons of the oil over medium-high heat. When the oil is hot, add the leeks and sprinkle with salt and pepper. Reduce the heat to medium and cook, stirring frequently, until the leeks begin to color, about 10 minutes. When the leeks are golden brown on the edges or beginning to stick to the pan, stir in the water to keep them from browning and to help them braise. Continue to cook until the liquid evaporates, the leeks are very tender, and the mixture has become the consistency of jam, 10 to 15 minutes. Transfer to a small bowl and set aside.

Using the same pan, add the remaining 2 tablespoons oil and return to medium-high heat. When the oil is hot, add the mushrooms, season with salt and pepper, and cook until they have released their juices, the juices have cooked off, and the mushrooms are caramelizing on the edges, about 20 minutes.

Meanwhile, shape the pizza crust as directed in the master recipe. Gently smear the leeks on top of the crust, being careful not to tear the dough and leaving about a 1-inch border all around—using the back of a spoon helps. Top the leeks with half of the Gruyère, all of the mushrooms, the thyme, and lastly, the remaining cheese.

Transfer the pizza to the oven and bake until the crust is browned and the cheese has melted, 6 to 10 minutes.

Whether you sauté, grill, roast, or braise them, leeks just always seem to be there with a buttery, silky, almost sweet disposition.

EGGPLANT, OREGANO, GOAT CHEESE, AND LEMONY GREENS

So in my fantasy I'm standing on a hill on a Greek Island. There are goats milling around under the olive trees, and the sun is sparkling on the sea like so many sequins on a slinky cocktail dress. The houses are those chalky white stucco cubes topped with terra-cotta tiles. Are you with me? The scenery is straight out of Summer Lovers circa 1982 (yes, that's the one with Daryl Hannah and Peter Gallagher) except instead of engaging in a ménage à trois, in my day-dream I'm eating pizza. This one to be exact. It includes pretty much everything I conjure up when I'm stuck in the city but would really rather be on a beach or a cliff in Santorini.

1 small eggplant
3 tablespoons extra virgin olive oil
Sea salt and freshly ground pepper
1 ball pizza dough (page 16), thawed if frozen
About 3 ounces goat cheese, sliced or crumbled
Leaves from 2 to 3 sprigs fresh oregano
About 2 handfuls baby arugula or watercress
Grated zest and juice of 1 lemon

Preheat the oven to 550°F.

Using a sharp knife or a mandoline, cut the eggplant lengthwise into very thin ribbons. Brush the eggplant on both sides with 2 tablespoons of the oil and sprinkle with salt and pepper.

Shape the pizza crust as directed in the master recipe. Scatter the goat cheese evenly over the crust, sprinkle with the oregano, and lay the eggplant slices on top of everything.

Transfer the pizza to the oven and bake until the crust is browned, the eggplant is tender and just coloring, and the cheese has melted, 6 to 10 minutes.

Meanwhile, in a medium bowl, toss the greens with the remaining table-spoon oil, the lemon zest, and lemon juice. Season with salt and pepper.

To serve, top the finished pizza with the dressed greens and return to the oven for 1 to 2 minutes to just barely wilt the greens.

CARAMELIZED FENNEL AND PEARS WITH STILTON

Full disclosure: I love cheese, and I really adore a nice stinky cheese. If I'm home alone, there's a good chance dinner will consist of a glass of good white, some kind of fruit (figs, dates, an apple, whatever), and a hunk of stinky cheese. Judge me as you will, but there's beauty and grace in this combination, and it translates perfectly to pizza. The caramelized fennel serves as the sweet-savory moderator to the bite of the Stilton and the sugar of the pear, meaning even if you claim to be a traditionalist like my husband (mostly mozzarella and no fruit on pizza), you may very well take exception here. If you do like this trio and want to play around, think Gorgonzola or any creamy blue paired with figs, apples, or even stone fruit like peaches and plums.

3 tablespoons extra virgin olive oil
1 bulb fennel, trimmed and thinly sliced, fronds reserved
Sea salt
¼ cup water
1 ball pizza dough (page 16), thawed if frozen
1 firm pear, very thinly sliced
About 3 ounces Stilton cheese, crumbled

Preheat the oven to 550°F.

In a medium saucepan, heat 2 tablespoons of the oil over medium-high heat. When the oil is hot, add the fennel and sprinkle with salt. Reduce the heat to medium and cook, stirring occasionally, until the fennel begins to color, 8 to 12 minutes. When the fennel is just turning brown on the edges, add the water, increase the heat to medium-high, and continue to cook until all the liquid has evaporated and the fennel is very tender and nicely colored, 10 to 12 minutes. Remove from the heat and let cool a bit.

Shape the pizza crust as directed in the master recipe. Gently spread the fennel evenly over the dough. In a small bowl, toss the pear slices with the remaining 1 tablespoon oil. Place the slices in concentric circles if you like, or just scatter them about randomly, then dot the pizza with the Stilton.

Transfer the pizza to the oven and bake until the crust is browned, the cheese has melted, and the pears are browning on the edges, 6 to 10 minutes.

MARINATED ARTICHOKES WITH SPINACH AND FETA

There's a place down on Bleecker Street we've been going to for years to buy our sausage, prosciutto, and olives called Faicco's Pork Store. The guys who work there are fabulous (they all look really young but have been there forever—it's one of the great mysteries of my shopping life), and their sweet fennel sausage is better than any I've ever tasted. They also have the very best marinated artichoke hearts on the planet—the kind with the long stems steeped in olive oil and just enough herby brine to enhance their artichoke-y flavor but not overpower it. When we buy these marinated thistles, it's a selfish treat for whoever is doing the cooking to nibble on the stems while slicing the hearts. If you can't find these delicacies, the ones in the jar are a passable substitute, but it won't be quite the same. Layered with Roma tomatoes, tangles of spinach, and crumbled feta cheese, this pizza may sound a little schizophrenic, like a mishmash of the Mediterranean, but it really works.

1 tablespoon extra virgin olive oil
1 container (5 ounces) baby spinach
Sea salt and freshly ground pepper
1 ball pizza dough (page 16), thawed if frozen
2 marinated artichokes with stems
1 Roma tomato, thinly sliced
About 3 ounces feta cheese, crumbled
Leaves from 2 sprigs fresh mint

Preheat the oven to 550°F.

In a large skillet or saucepan, heat the oil over medium-high heat. When the oil is hot, add the spinach, sprinkle with salt and pepper, and, using tongs and working quickly, sauté until just wilted, 2 to 3 minutes. Remove from the heat and set aside to cool. When the spinach is cool enough to handle, squeeze out as much liquid as possible (if it's not dry, the spinach will bleed out and make for a soggy crust).

Shape the pizza crust as directed in the master recipe. Slice the artichoke hearts lengthwise into quarters or even sixths. Lay the tomato evenly over the dough followed by the artichokes. Scatter the spinach evenly over the pizza. Top everything with the feta.

Transfer the pizza to the oven and bake until the crust is browned and the cheese has softened if not fully melted, 6 to 10 minutes. To serve, sprinkle with the mint.

SWEET POTATO AND SAGE WITH PECORINO

I have a sage plant I put in the first year we bought our cottage. That was the same year we had a blizzard on Christmas weekend and lost a very old, beautifully tortured-looking rhododendron tree to the cold. I have pictures from that year of both Ken and me waist-deep in white, well into March. It was like the end of the world was coming. But no matter how bad it got, that little sage plant didn't give in. Its leaves turned crisp and brown in the freezing temperatures, its stems all but black with frostbite; but once spring came, it rallied back and actually doubled in size. I've moved it three times since. The last time, at the end of a long day of gardening, I rather unceremoniously stuck it in a holding bed and never went back to find it a proper home. Yet it still keeps pushing out velvety, aromatic leaves in the most glorious blue-gray colors. As much as I neglect it, I am always thrilled to wander out and pull off a few furry leaves to make this pizza; the contrast of the smoky sage flavor with the sweet tuber is just sublime.

½ medium sweet potato, peeled and sliced
⅛ inch thick
3 tablespoons extra virgin olive oil
½ red onion, thinly sliced
Sea salt
¼ teaspoon red pepper flakes (or more to taste)

1 ball pizza dough (page 16), thawed if frozen
About 3 ounces fresh mozzarella cheese, torn into bite-size pieces
About 8 fresh sage leaves
¼ cup freshly grated pecorino cheese

Preheat the oven to 550°F.

Bring a pot of salted water to a boil. Add the sweet potato slices and cook until just tender on the edges but not soft or falling apart, 3 to 4 minutes. Drain in a colander and run under cold water immediately. Set aside.

In a medium skillet, heat 2 tablespoons of the oil over medium-high heat. When hot, add the onion, reduce the heat to medium, and season with salt and pepper flakes. Continue to cook, stirring occasionally, until soft and just beginning to color on the edges, 8 to 10 minutes. Remove from the heat.

Shape the pizza crust as directed in the master recipe. Evenly distribute the red onion over the top of the crust and scatter with the mozzarella. Add the sweet potato slices. Brush the sage leaves with the remaining tablespoon of oil and lay them over the potatoes. Sprinkle with the pecorino.

Transfer the pizza to the oven and bake until the crust is browned, the potato slices are crisp on the edges, and the cheese has melted, 6 to 10 minutes.

WHITE BEANS, ROSEMARY, CHARD, AND ROASTED GARLIC

My mom is a pretty fantastic cook (I know a lot of people say that about their moms, but mine really is). Growing up she didn't scour Gourmet magazine for fancy French dishes to dazzle us with; she just knew how to put ingredients together that worked. She also knew enough to rely on the right cookbooks for guidance. One of her go-to tomes (and mine to this day, though its pages are smeared and splattered and barely held together by a binder clip) is the Cafe Beaujolais cookbook. Café Beaujolais is a little spot on the coast of California in Mendocino. The ownership has changed now, but back in the early '80s, then-owner Margaret Fox put out a cookbook—a volume of recipes accompanied by her story of opening and running the restaurant, the food, and the customers she served. I've never been there, but for years I've loved reading her tale of starting the restaurant, and I've coveted her recipes. Her simple apple crumble recipe is burned into my brain, so I can whip it up on demand no matter where I am, and her lemon curd is flat-out wonderful. But it's her White Bean Goop (yes, that's what it's called) that my mom made as an appetizer when we were having company over that I love the most. A puree of beans, fresh rosemary, garlic, and lemon smeared on toasted bread—it's stunning. Maybe it's the recipe, maybe it's the way my mom makes it, but regardless, it's the inspiration for this pizza.

2 tablespoons extra virgin olive oil
½ bunch chard, cut into ribbons
¼ teaspoon red pepper flakes
Sea salt and freshly ground pepper
Half a 14-ounce can cannellini or other white beans, drained and rinsed
Leaves from 1 sprig fresh rosemary, finely chopped
Grated zest of 1 lemon
1 ball pizza dough (page 16), thawed if frozen
About 1 tablespoon Roasted Garlic Smear (page 29)
About 3 ounces fresh mozzarella cheese, torn into bite-size pieces

Preheat the oven to 550°F.

In a medium skillet, heat the oil over medium-high heat. Add the chard, sprinkle with the pepper flakes, and season with salt and pepper. Cook, stirring almost constantly, until the leaves are just wilted. Remove from the heat and let cool slightly. If it seems to need it, give it a squeeze to release any extra liquid (if you cook it fast enough, I find it usually doesn't).

In a small bowl, toss the beans with the rosemary and lemon zest, and season lightly with salt and pepper.

Shape the pizza crust as directed in the master recipe. Using the back of a spoon so as not to tear the dough, smear the roasted garlic evenly over the crust, leaving about a 1-inch border all around. Scatter the mozzarella over the garlic and spread the chard over the cheese layer (don't worry if you have little tangles here and there). Top everything with an even layer of the beans.

Transfer the pizza to the oven and bake until the crust is browned and the cheese has melted, 6 to 10 minutes.

My mom is a pretty fantastic cook (I know a lot of people say that about their moms, but mine really is). Growing up she didn't scour Gourmet magazine for fancy French dishes to dazzle us with; she just knew how to put ingredients together that worked.

MORELS WITH ASPARAGUS, TARRAGON, AND RICOTTA

"Springtime in the French Countryside" is really what I want to call this pizza. Earthy morels, grassy asparagus, licorice-y tarragon, and creamy ricotta all tumbled together—it's rich and luscious, yet somehow rustic and fresh at the same time. Admittedly, morels are extravagant (meaning expensive) and very seasonal. The lovely thing about them is the loamy flavor and honeycomb texture, but I'm not one to let rarified ingredients keep me from making dinner. Which is why I'm almost as happy to pick up fresh chanterelles or oyster mushrooms and not give it a second thought. Truthfully, even a handful of cremini would be serviceable. It's just a pizza after all.

½ bunch asparagus (8 to 10 spears)
1 tablespoon extra virgin olive oil
Sea salt and freshly ground pepper
2 tablespoons unsalted butter
1 shallot, finely chopped
1 cup halved fresh morels
Leaves from 2 or 3 sprigs fresh tarragon or chervil
1 ball pizza dough (page 16), thawed if frozen
About ½ cup whole-milk ricotta cheese

Preheat the oven to 400°F. Line a baking sheet with foil.

Trim the asparagus by holding a spear at both ends and bending it until it snaps. Discard the woody stem and either break them all this way, or break one and lay the rest together in a bundle and cut them all at the same level of the first. Place the asparagus on the baking sheet, drizzle with the oil, and sprinkle with salt and pepper. Roast until the asparagus is bright green and just tender, about 6 minutes. Remove from the oven and let sit. Leave the oven on and increase the temperature to 550°F.

In a medium skillet, melt the butter over medium-high heat. When the foam subsides, add the shallot and sauté for a minute or two. Add the mushrooms and cook, stirring occasionally, until they are just soft, about 5 minutes. Stir in the tarragon or chervil and season with salt and pepper.

Shape the pizza crust as directed in the master recipe. Use the back of a spoon to smear half of the ricotta over the crust, leaving about a 1-inch border all around. Spoon the mushroom mixture evenly over the ricotta. Add the roasted asparagus and dollop the remaining ricotta over the pizza.

Transfer the pizza to the oven and bake until the crust is golden brown, 6 to 10 minutes.

EGGPLANT, GOAT CHEESE, AND GREEN OLIVES

I love eggplant. Ken will eat it but doesn't really get it. I adore goat cheese. He won't go there. I could live on olives. Ken has grown to like them, sort of. So suffice it to say, this pizza is all about me. It's the selfish-pie, the one I make when I'm home alone and a purple globe is staring at me from the fruit bowl begging to be eaten before becoming bitter. It's a combination that makes me feel like I'm in Italy, deep in the countryside, olive trees as far as the eye can see, the scent of wood burning, and old stone houses dotting the hills, their splendor faded but still beautiful in that timeless way. When I close my eyes and bite into this pizza, that's my life. And it's perfect. It's only when I open my eyes that I'm reminded that I'm actually in my small kitchen in New York, wrangling three very ill-behaved cats, listening to sirens wail down Seventh Avenue, and realizing I forgot to buy milk. Damn. Luckily Ken is out (which is why I can eat this selfish meal), so he can pick some up on his way home.

1 medium eggplant, cut crosswise into ¼-inch-thick rounds
Olive oil, for brushing
Sea salt and freshly ground pepper
½ cup Cerignola, Picholine, Castelvetrano, or other green olives, pitted and halved
1 ball pizza dough (page 16), thawed if frozen
About 3 ounces goat cheese, crumbled
Leaves from 1 or 2 sprigs fresh oregano

Preheat the oven to 550°F. Heat a grill or grill pan until very hot.

Brush the eggplant slices with the oil and sprinkle with salt and pepper. When the grill is hot, working in batches if necessary, grill the eggplant until well-defined char lines appear on both sides and the flesh begins to soften, 2 to 3 minutes per side.

Shape the pizza crust as directed in the master recipe. Brush the top of the crust with olive oil, leaving about a 1-inch border all around. Place the grilled eggplant slices on the dough and scatter the olive halves evenly over the top. Sprinkle the goat cheese over the vegetables and top everything with oregano.

Transfer the pizza to the oven and bake until the crust is browned and the cheese has turned into creamy puddles, 6 to 10 minutes.

LEEK JAM WITH MIDSUMMER CORN

(aka Erica's Improvised Pizza)

When we finished building our pizza oven, the first people we had over were our friends Erica and Matt. As many of us are prone to do these days, at that inaugural dinner Erica posted some pictures on Instagram with a caption that read, "Life Advice: Make friends with someone who has an outdoor pizza oven. It rocks." As a close friend with an obvious affection for pizza and a sense of culinary adventure, Erica was the one I persuaded to be my partner in crime throughout the photo shoot for this book. For a week she and I made pizza after pizza based on the recipes I had concocted over the years. Then, on the last day of shooting, with the pizza oven blazing, a few unused balls of dough and random leftover toppings in the fridge, and a sense of giddy accomplishment in the air, Erica began making pizzas just for the hell of it. The first one she pulled together was ridiculously simple—a good smear of leftover leek jam dappled with buttery mozzarella and dotted with lots of sweet corn; it was pure improv, the pizza equivalent of Ella Fitzgerald scatting "How High the Moon." As if to punctuate the whole point of this book, she pulled it together spontaneously from just a few stray ingredients—and while there was barely anything to it, it was perfect. My life advice? Make friends with someone like Erica and eat lots of her glorious leek and corn pizza.

2 tablespoons extra virgin olive oil
1 large leek, cleaned and thinly sliced
Sea salt
1 ball pizza dough (page 16), thawed if frozen
About 3 ounces fresh mozzarella cheese, torn into bite-size pieces
1 ear of corn, kernels scraped off

Preheat the oven to 550°F.

In a medium skillet, heat the oil over medium-high heat until it shimmers. Add the leeks and sprinkle with salt. Reduce the heat to medium-low and cook, stirring frequently, until the leeks begin to soften, 10 to 12 minutes. Add a few tablespoons of water to the pan to keep them from browning and to help them braise. Continue to cook, stirring occasionally, until they meld together, 8 to 10 minutes (they should have an almost jam-like consistency).

Shape the pizza crust as directed in the master recipe. Spread the leeks evenly on the pizza crust using the back of a spoon, leaving about a 1-inch border all around and being careful not to tear the dough (you may very well have extra—freeze and save for later). Scatter the mozzarella over the leeks and then sprinkle the corn evenly over everything.

Transfer the pizza to the oven and bake until the crust is nicely browned and the cheese is melted, 6 to 10 minutes.

CURRIED CAULIFLOWER WITH TOMATOES AND CILANTRO

Certain flavors are destined to be together: tomatoes and basil, peas and mint, chicken and tarragon . . . and cauliflower and curry. Something about the way the warm spices of a robust curry powder cling to the ruffled, caramelized edges of the milky, nutty florets is completely seductive. And when they're tossed in a stew with coconut milk, you'd believe you were far off in a place where saffron grows and gilded minarets dot the landscape. Those same flavors on a pizza, paired with bright tomatoes and astringent cilantro, are equally as exotic yet somehow more mysterious. You're left wondering exactly where you and your taste buds have wandered off to—but you know you'd like to stay for more than just one slice.

½ small head cauliflower, cut into small florets
4 tablespoons extra virgin olive oil
Sea salt and freshly ground pepper
1 tablespoon curry powder (or more to taste)
1 ball pizza dough (page 16), thawed if frozen
½ small red onion, thinly sliced
1 Roma tomato, thinly sliced
¼ teaspoon red pepper flakes
Handful of fresh cilantro leaves

Preheat the oven to 400°F.

Place the cauliflower florets on a baking sheet and toss with 3 tablespoons of the oil and season with salt and pepper. Roast until the cauliflower is nicely colored and tender when pierced with a sharp knife, 20 to 30 minutes. Remove the cauliflower from the oven and increase the oven temperature to 550°F. Toss the cauliflower with the curry powder until evenly coated.

Shape the pizza crust as directed in the master recipe. Brush the dough evenly with the remaining 1 tablespoon oil, leaving about a 1-inch border all around. Scatter the red onion over the crust followed by the tomatoes. Spread the curried cauliflower over the onion and tomatoes. Sprinkle with the pepper flakes.

Transfer the pizza to the oven and bake until the crust is browned, the tomatoes have softened, and the onions are just coloring, 6 to 10 minutes. To serve, scatter the cilantro over the top of the pizza.

BROCCOLINI, MUSHROOM, AND CRUNCHY BREADCRUMBS

Another flagrant borrowing of flavors, this time from the impeccable taste of Yotam Ottolenghi. In his vegetarian cookbook Plenty, *he puts together a beautiful pasta of broccoli, mushrooms, and breadcrumbs with just a hint of a cream sauce. I first made this pasta of his when my sister and her husband, Jeremy, were visiting from San Francisco (both are vegetarians), and it quickly became one of our favorite weeknight pasta dinners. As a result, it was a no-brainer to try and re-create the textural and flavor combination on a pizza. The difference here of course is that to replicate the richness of cream, I use ricotta, and I like a bit of heat in my breadcrumbs, so I add red pepper flakes. I prefer broccolini over regular broccoli, but either works, and as for mushrooms, use what you have or what you like: button, cremini, shiitake, chanterelle, or a combination.*

Sea salt and freshly ground pepper
1 bunch broccolini, trimmed
2 tablespoons unsalted butter
2 cups quartered cremini or button mushrooms
½ cup fresh breadcrumbs
Pinch of red pepper flakes (or to taste)
1 tablespoon extra virgin olive oil
1 ball pizza dough (page 16), thawed if frozen
About ¼ cup whole-milk ricotta cheese
Grated zest of 1 lemon

Preheat the oven to 550°F.

Bring a pot of salted water to a boil. Add the broccolini and cook for 2 to 3 minutes. Pierce a stalk with a small sharp knife to make sure it is crisp-tender. Drain the broccolini and immediately run under cold water. Chop the broccolini into bite-size pieces (you'll likely have enough for two dinners here, so feel free to stash some in the freezer).

Meanwhile, in a medium skillet, melt the butter over medium-high heat. When the foam subsides, add the mushrooms, season with salt and black pepper, reduce the heat to medium, and cook, stirring occasionally. Continue to cook until the mushrooms release their juices and the liquid evaporates. Then cook until the edges of the mushrooms begin to caramelize, about 15 minutes total. Remove from the pan.

In a small bowl, combine the breadcrumbs, pepper flakes, and oil and toss. Season with salt.

Shape the pizza crust as directed in the master recipe. Smear the ricotta over the crust with the back of a spoon, leaving about a 1-inch border all around. Scatter the broccolini and mushrooms over the ricotta and sprinkle the breadcrumbs generously over all.

Transfer the pizza to the oven and bake until the crust is golden and the breadcrumbs are nicely browned, 6 to 10 minutes. To serve, sprinkle the lemon zest over the pizza.

Another flagrant borrowing of flavors, this time from the impeccable taste of Yotam Ottolenghi.

PEARS AND MAPLE-GLAZED PECANS WITH PECORINO

I love finding fruit in surprising places. When I was living in London just out of college, my uncle introduced me to a friend of his, Polly Bide. She was a terribly smart, sophisticated documentary producer with a fascinating life. Very nicely (and I'm sure only as a favor to my uncle), Polly invited me to her home for dinner one night. It was a hot English evening, and we sat on her terrace eating thick slices of whole-grain bread with a salad. On the surface the company was far more interesting than the food—but the salad was an utter revelation to me. I honestly don't remember anything special about it except for the raspberries. As I sat there, trying my best to sound slightly intelligent and remotely interesting, I was distracted: I couldn't stop focusing on the jewel-colored fruit mixed into the greens on my plate. I'd never had a savory salad with berries in it before. After that I became enamored of fruit in savory preparations. Apples sautéed with pancetta over greens, figs stuffed in a roasted pork loin, and yes, pears baked with syrupy pecans and salty sheep's milk cheese. Pecorino is what's often in my fridge, but a young Manchego is equally glorious. Polly died a few years ago at quite a young age, and while I only met her a couple of times, I will never forget that lovely midsummer night as an awkward 21-year-old in the presence of such a gracious and worldly woman—or the salad she served.

1 tablespoon unsalted butter
1 tablespoon maple syrup
½ teaspoon sea salt, plus more as needed
½ cup pecan halves, toasted
1 firm pear, very thinly sliced
1 ball pizza dough (page 16), thawed if frozen
2 ounces pecorino cheese, thinly sliced
Freshly ground pepper

Preheat the oven to 550°F.

In a small skillet, melt the butter over medium-high heat. When the foam subsides, add the syrup and salt and mix well. Add the toasted pecans and toss to coat evenly. Remove from the heat and transfer the pecans to a small dish. Add the pears to the pan with the syrupy liquid and gently toss to coat.

Shape the pizza crust as directed in the master recipe. Lay the cheese evenly over the crust and then top with the pear slices.

Transfer the pizza to the oven and bake until the crust is browned, the pears have softened, and the cheese has melted, 6 to 10 minutes. To serve, scatter the glazed pecans all over and sprinkle with the pepper.

OLIVE, GIGANTE BEANS, AND PRESERVED LEMON SALAD

We tend to eat a salad with our pizza—it somehow rounds out the meal. Even if it's just a nice bowl of lightly dressed greens or some combination of tomatoes and cucumbers drizzled with olive oil and sea salt. But some nights we look at each other and one of us says, "Do you want a salad? I can make a salad if you want one, but I could probably skip it." And most often the other person agrees and the salad is, somewhat sacrilegiously, skipped. This happens mostly when it's either very late or the pizza of the day is such that a salad feels redundant. This is one of those pizzas. The bright preserved lemons tossed with creamy beans and spicy arugula is a salad in and of itself—the pizza is just a very tasty plate.

1 can (14 ounces) gigante beans, drained and rinsed
½ cup Cerignola, Picholine, Castelvetrano, or other good-quality green olives, pitted and chopped
¼ to ½ cup Preserved Lemons (page 30)
1 to 2 tablespoons extra virgin olive oil, plus more for brushing
Leaves from 1 or 2 sprigs fresh oregano, finely chopped
Sea salt and freshly ground pepper
1 ball pizza dough (page 16), thawed if frozen
About 3 ounces fresh mozzarella cheese, torn into bite-size pieces
A few handfuls of baby arugula

Preheat the oven to 550°F.

In a medium bowl, combine the beans, olives, lemons, and oil (the mixture should be just lightly dressed). Add the oregano and stir gently. Taste the beans and season as needed (the lemons can be quite flavorful, so definitely do not salt until after you've tasted everything together).

Shape the pizza crust as directed in the master recipe. Brush it evenly with olive oil, leaving about a 1-inch border all around. Scatter the mozzarella evenly over the crust.

Transfer the pizza to the oven and bake until the crust is browned and the cheese has melted, 6 to 10 minutes.

Meanwhile, toss the arugula with the beans, allowing the greens to wilt slightly in the oil and acid of the lemons.

When the pizza is done, scoop the salad onto the pizza and spread it evenly over the top. To serve, sprinkle with freshly ground pepper.

CHARCUTERIE
and MEAT
PIZZAS

I know I've made this point already, but we don't consume a huge amount of meat in our house. It's not something we have to think about, it's just the way we eat, and I attribute it largely to our pizza habit. Ken does like meat, and growing up with a German mother who was a traditionalist in the kitchen, he was raised to expect dinner to be built around some sort of a protein, usually a roast chicken or a pot roast. The beauty of pizza, however, is that dinner is built around the crust—followed of course by whatever bibs and bobs go on top. Which is why we eat small amounts of meat—a single sausage shared by two, four thin slices of prosciutto, a cup of ground lamb—but do so relatively regularly.

The most important thing I've learned about pizza when it comes to meat is this: Less is definitely better than more. I love prosciutto, I love bresaola (air-dried, salted beef that's aged—I think of it as prosciutto from a cow), I love pancetta and bacon, shredded pork, ground lamb or meatballs, but I don't need very much of any of these on a pizza to feel completely satiated. When it comes to pizza, there is so much going on, so many layers of flavor—from the crust to the sauce to all the toppings—that you don't want one single ingredient to overwhelm the rest. And meat has a way of being that potentially dominant ingredient.

My rule when making a pizza that uses meat is to think of it as a seasoning. A handful of pancetta or bacon is more than enough to provide a smoky, meaty, salty essence to a pie (and if you use the fat from cooking it as a smear on the crust, you get even more flavor out of that handful). A few crumbles of a single sausage are enough for your brain to register the flavor without letting the radicchio, fennel, sweet onion, or other delicious sidekick get drowned out. Generally speaking, a little meat goes a long way—which means that tossing an extra chicken breast on the grill or a pork chop in the pan is all you need to do to have enough leftover meat for pizza dinner later in the week.

Certainly a pizza doesn't need meat to be delicious. But when prosciutto slices lay draped across minty basil leaves, milky burrata, and just-picked cherry tomatoes in a come-hither fashion, it's hard to resist their allure.

PROSCIUTTO, BASIL, BLACK OLIVE, AND SAN MARZANO TOMATOES

This is my fallback no-muss, no-fuss combo (aka the "I-just-walked-in-but-dinner-will-be-ready-in-mere-minutes" pizza). When I'm craving the comfort of a homemade pizza but don't have the inclination to do much more than deal with stretching out a crust, it's a lifesaver, requiring no more effort than a mad dash into the grocery store on the way home. There's virtually no prepping (it's all in the shopping), and you don't even need a knife—just a can opener and you're set. If you're efficient, dinner will be on the table 20 minutes after your oven is hot. If you stop to pour a glass of wine first (as you should), it may be closer to 25.

1 ball pizza dough (page 16), thawed if frozen
4 or 5 canned San Marzano tomatoes
About 3 ounces fresh mozzarella cheese, torn into bite-size pieces
¼ cup Kalamata olives, pitted
Fresh basil leaves, torn into pieces
4 to 6 slices prosciutto di Parma

Preheat the oven to 550°F.

Shape the pizza crust as directed in the master recipe.

Squeeze the juice and as many of the seeds as you can out of the canned tomatoes, and then tear each tomato into 3 or 4 pieces each. Place them randomly on the crust. Scatter the mozzarella on the pie along with the olives and basil. Lay the prosciutto evenly over the other ingredients.

Transfer the pizza to the oven and bake until the crust is nicely browned, the prosciutto is slightly toasted, and the cheese is bubbling, 6 to 10 minutes.

(aka the "I-just-walked-in-but-dinner-will-be-ready-in-mere-minutes" pizza)

CHORIZO WITH SPINACH AND CHICKPEAS

Ken and I took a trip to southern Spain once, and we fell hard for tapas. We're both grazers, though I'm definitely worse than he is. Weekend lunches at our house are often a messy counter laden with various nubs of cheese, crackers or a hunk of bread, a dish of salted olive oil maybe, some thick slices of saucisson or thin sheets of Serrano ham. All of which is to say, the locally endorsed practice of snacking with a glass in hand in Seville and Granada suited us perfectly; we both enjoyed the rhythm of eating—a bit here, a bite there—as much as the vibrant, lush flavors. I think of this pizza as a dalliance with Spain, kind of like spilling a few of the tapas dishes onto a crust and discovering something wonderful.

2 tablespoons extra virgin olive oil
½ cup sliced dry-cured chorizo sausage
1 cup canned chickpeas, drained and rinsed
1 container (5 ounces) baby spinach
Sea salt and freshly ground pepper
1 ball pizza dough (page 16), thawed if frozen
¼ cup freshly shaved Manchego cheese

Preheat the oven to 550°F.

In a large skillet, heat 1 tablespoon of the oil over medium-high heat. Add the chorizo and reduce the heat to medium. Cook the chorizo for about 5 minutes, stirring occasionally, until some of the fat from the sausage has rendered. Add the chickpeas, toss to coat them in the spicy oil, and cook until the chorizo begins to brown on the edges, another 3 minutes or so. Using a slotted spoon, transfer the chorizo and chickpeas to a bowl. Reserve the fat from the skillet in another small bowl.

In the same skillet, heat the remaining 1 tablespoon oil over high heat. When the oil is hot, add the spinach, sprinkle with salt and pepper, and cook, tossing frequently, until just wilted, about 2 minutes. Remove the spinach from the heat and let sit until cool enough to handle. Squeeze the spinach to drain off any excess liquid.

Shape the pizza crust as directed in the master recipe. Brush the surface with the reserved chorizo fat, leaving about a 1-inch border all around. Sprinkle the chorizo and chickpeas evenly over the crust and then drop small tangles of spinach over the sausage and beans.

Transfer the pizza to the oven and bake until the crust is nicely browned and the chickpeas are beginning to toast, 6 to 10 minutes. To serve, top the pizza with the Manchego shavings and freshly ground pepper.

PEPPERONI AND KALAMATA OLIVES WITH POMODORO SAUCE

For a very short period of time in college I worked at a pizzeria. I was a delivery girl (person, I suppose, is the right way to say that) but I was not very good at it. One day I got to work behind the counter with the pizza maker and learned a couple of useful things: Always spread sauce with the back of a spoon. Start by pooling a bit in the middle and working outward in concentric circles. Don't use too much. Along with these valuable tidbits of pizza-making expertise, I was also afforded the very exciting perk of a free small pie with each shift. For some reason, during this time of free pizza, I was obsessed with pepperoni and olives as a combination. I'd like to say there was a very high-minded culinary reason for it, but the truth is, I just liked how the pepperoni got crisp on the edges, how the little glistening pools of orange oil gathered in places, and how the canned black olives (for they most certainly were) tasted against that backdrop. I don't do pepperoni often these days, but when I do, this is the nostalgic little number I like to throw together, sauce always spread with the back of a spoon.

1 ball pizza dough (page 16), thawed if frozen
¼ cup Essential Pomodoro Sauce (page 25)
About 3 ounces fresh mozzarella cheese, torn into bite-size pieces
10 to 12 slices pepperoni
½ cup pitted Kalamata olives, halved

Preheat the oven to 550°F.

Shape the pizza crust as directed in the master recipe. Using the back of a spoon so the crust doesn't tear, spread the sauce evenly over the dough, leaving about a 1-inch border all around. Scatter the mozzarella over the sauce. Lay the pepperoni over the cheese and then spread the olives on top.

Transfer the pizza to the oven and bake until the crust is nicely browned and the cheese has melted, 6 to 10 minutes.

RED ONION, PANCETTA, PINE NUTS, AND RICOTTA

One of the perks of my job as a food stylist is leftovers—after a photo shoot, everyone shares in the bounty. It's also one of the more absurd parts of my job: As the one who has to make sure the kitchen is cleaned up at the end of it all, I find myself left to deal with the odds and ends. If you open my pantry at any given time, you'll see three containers of baking powder (maybe four); five boxes of dark brown sugar (but no light brown, for some odd reason); an inordinate amount of coconut milk (full fat and light); more mirin, soy sauce, and sesame oil than you can fathom; and don't get me started on my spice collection. I also find myself with more pine nuts than any one family needs—in a lifetime. Especially a family that really doesn't use a lot of pine nuts. But they're nice to have on hand (I keep them in the freezer so they don't go rancid), and they add a luscious buttery crunch to this pizza. Along with the salty pork, sweet-almost-burnt onion, and milky cheese, they bring something special to this simple pie.

3 to 4 tablespoons extra virgin olive oil
¼ pound pancetta, cut into ¼-inch pieces
½ medium red onion, thinly sliced
1 ball pizza dough (page 16), thawed if frozen
About ½ cup whole-milk ricotta cheese
¼ cup pine nuts, toasted

Preheat the oven to 550°F.

In a medium skillet, heat 2 tablespoons of the oil over medium-high heat. When the oil is hot, add the pancetta. Reduce the heat to medium and cook, stirring occasionally, until the pancetta begins to color but isn't crisp. Use a slotted spoon to transfer the pancetta to a small bowl and set aside.

Place the same skillet (with the fat from the pancetta) over medium-high heat to cook the onion, adding an extra 1 or 2 tablespoons olive oil if necessary. When hot, add the onions, reduce the heat to medium, and cook, stirring occasionally, until they are very soft and beginning to color a bit, 8 to 12 minutes. Then increase the heat to high to let the onions color just a bit more—you don't want them to burn, but you do want the ends to go almost crisp. Remove from the heat.

Shape the pizza crust as directed in the master recipe. Using the back of a spoon, smear half of the ricotta over the crust in an even layer, leaving about a 1-inch border all around. Gently spread the tangle of onions over the ricotta in a thin layer and sprinkle with the pancetta bits and pine nuts. Top with small dollops of the remaining ricotta.

Transfer the pizza to the oven and bake until the crust is nicely browned and the cheese has softened, 6 to 10 minutes.

ARTICHOKE, SERRANO HAM, AND ROMA TOMATO

You've probably noticed that I borrow wildly from cooks I love, this recipe included. About a hundred years ago, I was given a book called Bistro Cooking *by the amazing Patricia Wells. I was probably only 22 and I was smitten with how perfect her recipes were. I adored the idea that I was now making real French bistro food at home with a guide as thoughtful and knowledgeable as Ms. Wells. Soon I found my way to her follow-up,* Trattoria, *and again followed her with total confidence, a dedication that was sealed one night when I needed to pull dinner together with barely anything in the fridge. I had about five things lying around and happily three of them were all I needed to make one of her remarkable pastas: marinated artichoke hearts, Roma tomatoes, and prosciutto. On the table in less time than it's taken to share this story (well, almost), this dish has been a family go-to for quick dinners for years. Then one day the ingredients simply pleaded to live on a crust instead of in a bowl of penne. No surprise, it worked like a charm.*

1 ball pizza dough (page 16), thawed if frozen
1 Roma tomato, thinly sliced
About 3 ounces fresh mozzarella cheese, torn into bite-size pieces
2 to 3 marinated artichoke hearts with the stem, sliced
4 to 6 slices Serrano ham or proscuitto

Preheat the oven to 550°F.

Shape the pizza crust as directed in the master recipe.

Lay the tomato slices evenly over the crust and scatter the mozzarella on top. Place the artichoke pieces evenly over the crust and then tear the ham into strips and spread over everything.

Transfer the pizza to the oven and bake until the crust is nicely browned and the cheese has melted, 6 to 10 minutes.

ASPARAGUS AND FRIED EGGS WITH GUANCIALE

For a little over a year, Ken and I lived in an old house on the beach in Connecticut because of his job. It was a quirky old place with a view of the water from the kitchen and a completely overgrown vegetable garden that hadn't been touched in years. Our landlord said we could do whatever we liked to the garden as long as we didn't tear out the established asparagus bed nestled off to one side of the patch. At the time, we couldn't see evidence of said bed, but with some weeding and care, we rather quickly found ourselves with fresh asparagus stalks poking up from the ground regularly. Sometimes it seemed almost overnight those green stems would rise up and be ready for harvesting by dinner. We loved those fresh spears, some pencil-thin and others thick as thumbs—so much so, in fact, that this season we planted our own small bed in the corner of our yard, in hopes that in a year or so we'll have our own asparagus. And when we do, this will be the first pizza I make.

½ bunch asparagus (8 to 10 spears)
3 to 4 tablespoons extra virgin olive oil
Sea salt and freshly ground pepper
¼ pound guanciale (Italian cured pork cheeks or jowl) or pancetta, diced (about ½ cup)
1 ball pizza dough (page 16), thawed if frozen
About 3 ounces fresh mozzarella cheese, torn into bite-size pieces
2 large eggs

Preheat the oven to 400°F.

Trim the asparagus by holding the spears at both ends and bending them until they break. This is the sweet spot, and you can discard the woody stem once the spear has snapped. If you're devoted, do break them all this way. If you're in a hurry, break one and lay the rest together in a bundle, and cut them all at the same level of the first.

Spread the asparagus out on a baking sheet, drizzle with 2 tablespoons of the oil, sprinkle with salt, and toss to coat. Roast until bright green and just tender, 5 to 7 minutes. Remove from the oven and set aside. Increase the oven temperature to 550°F.

Meanwhile, in a medium skillet, heat 1 tablespoon of the oil over medium-high heat. When the oil is hot, add the guanciale, reduce the heat to medium, and cook, stirring occasionally, until browned but not crisp, about 6 minutes. Transfer the guanciale to a bowl but keep the fat in the pan.

Shape the pizza crust as directed in the master recipe. Brush a bit of the remaining fat over the crust, if you like, and scatter the mozzarella over the top along with the guanciale. Either lay the whole roasted asparagus randomly over the pie or cut the asparagus into 2-inch pieces and scatter over the pie.

Transfer the pizza to the oven and bake until the crust is nicely browned and the cheese has melted, 6 to 10 minutes.

Meanwhile, heat the reserved fat from the guanciale over medium heat, adding a bit more olive oil if needed. When the oil is hot, fry the eggs until the whites are just set but the yolks are still loose, 3 to 4 minutes. To serve, top the pizza with the fried eggs and a sprinkle of sea salt and freshly ground pepper.

We loved those fresh spears, some pencil-thin and others thick as thumbs.

BROCCOLI RABE WITH SOPPRESSATA AND AN EGG

Many years ago there was a place on the corner of Jane Street and 8th Avenue, just a block from our apartment, called Freddy's. It was that rare thing you don't find very often in New York these days: a small, family-run Italian restaurant that served really delicious food. Freddy was there every night, either taking orders or checking to make sure everyone was enjoying themselves. One night we called and asked if they'd deliver; we were only slightly surprised to find Freddy himself standing with steaming containers at our door within the hour. I could be wrong here, but I'm pretty sure Freddy's was the first place I ever had broccoli rabe. I don't know if it wasn't fashionable yet or if I'd just missed the boat, but one night, probably our first or second visit, Freddy suggested we try the special appetizer. We gamely agreed. What he set before us was a twisted tumble of inky-green leaves, stalks, and florets dotted with cubes of homemade soppressata. It was beautiful in its austerity, yet the flavors were far from simple. I was besotted. Since that night broccoli rabe has gone from an exotic discovery to an everyday staple in our house. We never knew why Freddy's closed (restaurants can be so good and yet so fleeting in the city), but we miss it. I suppose this pizza is a kind of thank-you card to Freddy— and a love letter to one of my favorite vegetables.

Sea salt
½ bunch broccoli rabe
1 ball pizza dough (page 16), thawed if frozen
2 tablespoons extra virgin olive oil
About 3 ounces fresh mozzarella cheese, torn into bite-size pieces
¼ pound soppressata, diced (about ½ cup)
1 large egg
Freshly ground pepper

Preheat the oven to 550°F.

Bring a large pot of salted water to a boil. Add the broccoli rabe, stir, and cook until the water returns to a boil, the rabe is bright green, and the stems are barely tender. Drain and run under cold water to stop the cooking process. Let cool and then squeeze to remove any excess liquid.

Shape the pizza crust as directed in the master recipe. Brush 1 tablespoon of the oil over the crust and scatter the mozzarella over the top. Drape the broccoli rabe randomly over the pie and add the soppressata.

Transfer the pizza to the oven and bake until the crust is nicely browned and the cheese has melted, 6 to 10 minutes.

Heat the remaining 1 tablespoon oil in a skillet over medium heat. Fry the egg until the white is just set but the yolk is still loose, 3 to 4 minutes. To serve, top the pizza with the egg and a sprinkle of sea salt and pepper.

CARAMELIZED ONION AND PANCETTA WITH PARMESAN

Here's the thing about food styling for a living. After each shoot, you end up with bits and pieces of all kinds of things in your fridge. Often these are truly wonderful delicacies you're incredibly lucky to come by—a 3-inch-thick tomahawk steak, a tiny pouch of fresh morels, maybe a lump of beautiful cheese. And often as not, they're a really off-the-wall collection of leftovers you just feel bad about throwing away, so you take them home, telling yourself you'll use them before they go off. Which is how this pizza (and more than a few others in the book) came to be. Getting home from work one night and unpacking the remnants of the day, I was faced with a sweet onion, a hunk of pancetta, and a rather ridiculous amount of already grated Parmesan. Odds and ends that would either live out their days waiting for me to figure out how to use them or, better, get quickly whipped up into that night's pizza dinner.

2 tablespoons extra virgin olive oil
¼ pound pancetta, diced (about ½ cup)
½ Vidalia or other sweet onion, sliced in half-moons
2 to 3 tablespoons water
1 ball pizza dough (page 16), thawed if frozen
About 3 ounces fresh mozzarella cheese, torn into bite-size pieces
¼ cup freshly grated Parmesan cheese

Preheat the oven to 550°F.

In a medium skillet, heat 1 tablespoon of the oil over medium-high heat. When the oil is hot, reduce the heat to medium, add the pancetta, and cook, stirring occasionally, until it is browned but not crisp, 6 to 8 minutes. Use a slotted spoon to remove the pancetta and set aside. Pour off all but a tablespoon of the fat and set it aside in a small bowl.

Using the same pan, add the remaining 1 tablespoon oil to the pancetta fat and turn the heat back to medium-high. Add the onions, reduce the heat to medium, and cook, stirring occasionally, until they begin to soften and color, 6 to 8 minutes. Add the water to the pan to keep the onions from browning and to help them braise. Continue to cook, stirring occasionally (and adding more water, a tablespoon or so at a time, if they become dry), until they're nicely colored and have melded together, another 8 to 10 minutes. Use a slotted spoon to transfer the onions to a bowl.

Shape the pizza crust as directed in the master recipe. Brush the crust with the reserved pancetta fat, leaving about a 1-inch border all around. Spread the onion evenly over the crust using the back of a spoon. Scatter the mozzarella over the onion along with the pancetta. Sprinkle the Parmesan over the entire pie.

Transfer the pizza to the oven and bake until the crust is nicely browned and the cheese has melted, 6 to 10 minutes.

Getting home from work one night and unpacking the remnants of the day, I was faced with a sweet onion, a hunk of pancetta, and a rather ridiculous amount of already grated Parmesan.

BACON AND EGGS WITH BLACK PEPPER AND CHIVES

Breakfast for dinner is hardly a new thought. Growing up, Ken says his mom used to make him French toast for dinner when she was going out in the evening. My mom has been known to scramble up some eggs for a light, last-minute dinner as well. And who hasn't stood over the sink with a bowl of cereal in hand after a long day when the idea of cooking is just too much to bear? To my mind the Italians mastered the breakfast-as-dinner combo with carbonara— that irresistible tangle of creamy eggs, salty bacon, and spicy pepper. I adore carbonara, and this pizza puts that sublime combination on a great crust. Come to think of it, this would be a perfect breakfast pizza if one were so inclined.

2 tablespoons extra virgin olive oil
2 slices thick-cut bacon, cut into thirds
1 ball pizza dough (page 16), thawed if frozen
¼ cup Caramelized Onion Jam (page 27)
Fresh chives
2 large eggs
Sea salt and freshly ground pepper

Preheat the oven to 550°F.

In a large skillet, heat 1 tablespoon of the oil over medium-high heat. When the oil is hot, add the bacon, reduce the heat to medium, and cook, turning once or twice, until browned but not crisp, about 8 minutes. Transfer the bacon to a plate (don't feel compelled to blot it with paper towels) and reserve the bacon fat.

Shape the pizza crust as directed in the master recipe. Brush the crust with some of the reserved bacon fat, leaving about a 1-inch border all around. Gently spread the caramelized onion evenly over the crust, lay the chives randomly over the onion mixture, and top with the bacon.

Transfer the pizza to the oven and bake until the crust is nicely browned, 6 to 10 minutes.

Meanwhile, in a large skillet, heat the remaining 1 tablespoon oil over medium-high heat (or use the skillet from the bacon and a bit of the bacon fat—if there's enough, you can skip adding the olive oil). Add the eggs and cook for about 4 minutes, gently spooning any extra fat in the pan over them to help them set up. They are done when the whites are fully set but the yolks still wiggle.

To serve, transfer the eggs to the top of the pizza and sprinkle with sea salt and lots of freshly ground pepper.

PROSCIUTTO, ROASTED ASPARAGUS, AND FRESH PEAS WITH PARMESAN

Okay, time to pay homage to one of my favorite cooks—Nigella Lawson. No, her food isn't fussy. No, I don't love all her recipes. But damn if she isn't happy in the kitchen and sexy while she cooks. Long before I went to culinary school, I'd learned more than a few really useful kitchen tricks from Ms. Lawson, including how to make fantastic risi e bisi. If you're not familiar, risi e bisi is an Italian risotto with peas. Most recipes I've seen are basic white risottos that rely on just-picked fresh peas to bring them to life. Not so with Nigella's: She makes a rich pea sauce that she then adds to the risotto at the end, resulting in a vivid green pot of rice dotted with plump peas and alive with flavor. I took this concept and used it as a pasta sauce for years, until one day I had some leftover and smeared it on a pizza with delightful results. Some extra peas, a few torn slices of prosciutto, and extra Parmesan and you have my version of pizza e bisi. (This recipe will make more sauce than you need for one pizza, but it freezes well. Save the extra for another pie or to toss with pasta or risotto. Or, you could also just increase the proportions and serve this sauce as a chilled or warm soup. It's that good—a toasty crouton or some prosciutto crisps on top would be a nice touch.) And yes, this is a recipe where a box of frozen peas is just fine.

½ bunch asparagus (8 to 10 spears), trimmed
2 tablespoons extra virgin olive oil
Sea salt and freshly ground pepper
4 tablespoons unsalted butter, at room temperature
2 cups fresh or frozen peas
½ cup chicken stock
1 cup freshly grated Parmesan cheese
1 ball pizza dough (page 16), thawed if frozen
4 to 6 slices prosciutto, torn into bite-size pieces

Preheat the oven to 400°F.

Spread the asparagus out on a baking sheet. Drizzle with the oil, sprinkle with salt and pepper, and toss to coat. Roast until bright green and just tender, 5 to 7 minutes. Remove from the oven, set aside, and increase the oven temperature to 550°F.

Meanwhile, in a medium saucepan, melt 1 tablespoon of the butter over medium-high heat. Add the peas and swirl to coat them in the butter, then add the chicken stock. Bring the stock to a simmer and cook just until the peas turn bright green, 1 or 2 minutes. Remove the pan from the heat.

continued

continued

Use a slotted spoon to transfer half the peas to a bowl and set aside. Put the remaining peas and their cooking liquid in a food processor or blender (I use a mini food processor here) and puree. Add the remaining 3 tablespoons butter and ½ cup of the Parmesan and continue to process until smooth. Season with salt and pepper.

Shape the pizza crust as directed in the master recipe. Using the back of a spoon, gently smear the crust with the pea sauce, leaving about a 1-inch border all around. Cut the asparagus into 1-inch pieces and scatter them over the crust along with the reserved whole peas and the prosciutto. Finally, sprinkle the remaining ½ cup Parmesan over everything.

Transfer the pizza to the oven and bake until the crust is nicely browned and the cheese has melted, 6 to 10 minutes.

Some extra peas, a few torn slices of prosciutto, and extra Parmesan and you have my version of pizza e bisi.

SPICY SHREDDED PORK WITH SWEET ONION JAM AND BURRATA

There's something about slow-cooked sweet-and-spicy pork that's just heavenly. You know it can't be good for you, you know you shouldn't eat too much of it, but it's just the bees knees, so who can resist? We make a really simple slow-cooked pork that relies on nothing more than a great spice rub and a low-and-slow stint in the oven to produce a very large amount of tender, self-shredding, sweet-spicy-salty-porky sublimity. The truth is Ken is usually the one maneuvering this onto the menu (he's less hung up on keeping our pork intake in check than I am), and we mostly make it as a filling for tacos or even tamales and then use the leftovers for pizza. But how can one write a pizza book and leave out one of the best combos simply because it's a bit of work? Not possible. So first make our spicy shredded pork on page 212. However, if you're just not up for a bit of project cooking and want an abridged version, here's a cheat: Buy a chop or two. Rub the meat well with the same spice mixture as for the shredded pork, and grill or sear the chops. Then tear the meat up to approximate a shredded consistency and toss it with some more of the rub to really coat the meat in flavor. It's a shortcut for sure, but chances are you'll barely be able to tell you didn't slow-roast the whole hog. You can of course also use whatever leftover pork you have on hand.

1 ball pizza dough (page 16), thawed if frozen
½ to 1 cup shredded Slow-Cooked Sweet-and-Spicy Pork (page 212)
¼ cup Caramelized Onion Jam (page 27), made with Vidalia or other sweet onions
1 Roma tomato, thinly sliced
1 medium ball burrata

Preheat the oven to 550°F.

Shape the pizza crust as directed in the master recipe.

If you're feeling decadent, brush some of the fatty juices leftover from the pork over the crust. If not, simply smear the sweet onion jam over the surface of the dough, leaving about a 1-inch border all around. Lay the tomato slices over the onion and spread the shredded pork over the tomatoes.

Transfer the pizza to the oven and bake until the crust is nicely golden and the edges of the pork are beginning to crisp a bit, 6 to 10 minutes. About 1 minute before it's done, slide the pizza out of the oven and dollop each quarter with the burrata. Return the pizza to the oven for a minute just to let the burrata warm and melt slightly.

BRESAOLA, ARUGULA, AND PARMESAN

I'd never been to Rome until a couple of years ago. But I'd read somewhere that the skyline was virtually unchanged since early days and I was captivated by the notion of sultry afternoons wandering cobblestone streets, taking in the crumbling ruins, and watching the sophisticated and stylish Romans zip by on their ubiquitous Vespas. Yet, as excited as I was to see the city, I was still more excited to taste it. Armed with a list of markets, restaurants, gelaterias, and pizzerias from my most trusted food-focused friends, I set out to eat pizza bianca for breakfast and pasta carbonara for dinner, with a stop for something tantalizing and authentically Italian in between. That in-between meal turned out to be a salad of chiffon-thin bresaola (cured beef), spicy arugula, and shavings of Parmesan drizzled with golden green olive oil. It was a divine combination, and I ate it every chance I got until we headed to the airport and back to real life.

1 ball pizza dough (page 16), thawed if frozen
2 tablespoons extra virgin olive oil
About 3 ounces fresh mozzarella cheese, torn into bite-size pieces
6 to 8 slices bresaola
A handful of baby arugula
Juice of ½ lemon
Sea salt and freshly ground pepper
Freshly shaved Parmesan cheese

Preheat the oven to 550°F.

Shape the pizza crust as directed in the master recipe.

Brush the top of the crust with 1 tablespoon of the oil, leaving about a 1-inch border all around. Drop torn pieces of the mozzarella over the crust and then lay the bresaola evenly over the cheese.

Transfer the pizza to the oven and bake until the crust is nicely browned and the cheese has melted, 6 to 10 minutes.

Meanwhile, in a bowl, toss the arugula with the remaining 1 tablespoon of oil, the lemon juice, and salt and pepper to taste.

To serve, top the pizza with the dressed arugula and lots of shaved Parmesan.

GROUND LAMB WITH CUMIN, GRAPE TOMATOES, AND CILANTRO

I kind of hate the idea of a "Mexican pizza," a "Southwest pizza," or a "Hawaiian pizza." Labeling food by an entire location just feels like something you'd see on an oversized laminated menu at a theme restaurant. That said, I'd be lying if I didn't say this could probably be called a Middle Eastern or Greek-style pizza. The cumin-scented lamb definitely goes that way—the tomatoes, feta, and lemon, too. Alas, it's a great combination, despite the potential for a really terrible name.

2 tablespoons extra virgin olive oil
½ red onion, sliced
Sea salt and freshly ground pepper
½ pound ground lamb (or lamb shoulder finely chopped)
1 tablespoon ground cumin
2 good handfuls of fresh cilantro leaves, half chopped, half left whole
1 ball pizza dough (page 16), thawed if frozen
½ cup halved grape tomatoes
½ cup crumbled feta cheese
½ lemon

Preheat the oven to 550°F.

In a large skillet, heat the oil over medium-high heat. Add the onion, sprinkle with salt and pepper, reduce the heat to medium, and cook, stirring occasionally, until soft, about 5 minutes. Add the lamb and continue to cook until the meat is just browning, about 4 minutes. Add the cumin and chopped cilantro and toss to combine. Remove from the heat.

Shape the pizza crust as directed in the master recipe. Spread the lamb mixture evenly over the top of the crust, leaving about a 1-inch border all around. Scatter the tomatoes over the lamb.

Transfer the pizza to the oven and bake until the crust is nicely browned, 6 to 10 minutes. To serve, sprinkle the remaining whole cilantro leaves and the feta over the pie, then squeeze the lemon over everything.

BROCCOLI RABE PESTO, SWEET ITALIAN SAUSAGE, AND PARMESAN

One thing I've learned about food is that you can think you know a lot and then suddenly realize that you were actually missing out on a glaringly obvious and amazing combination of flavors, something so perfect that it's already a classic to almost everyone else in the known universe—and you had no idea. That's how I was with broccoli rabe, sweet sausage, and orecchiette. I was in my late twenties before I stumbled on this remarkable trio, but once I tasted it I was smitten. It's a little scary to think about how many bowls of broccoli rabe and sausage pasta I've made over the years (with a bit of white wine, pepper flakes, rosemary, and a good hunk of butter, it's as comforting as a hug after a rough day). But when you're cooking for two, there's always a bit too much rabe in a bunch and one sausage extra on hand, so I've taken to layering it on pizza like it was going out of style. Acknowledging that it has lately become rather trendy (and ubiquitous) to turn the broccoli rabe into pesto, I have to say it just makes sense for a pizza—you want a smear of that grassy flavor to coat the crust. And a few extra tender florets add great texture. The rabe does seem to get stronger and more intense in flavor when it's blitzed up into a pesto, so taste it to decide how much you want to smear on your crust. You'll definitely have enough to freeze for future pies.

Sea salt
1 bunch broccoli rabe, trimmed
¼ cup pistachios, walnuts, or pine nuts
6 tablespoons extra virgin olive oil, plus more as needed
1 cup freshly grated Parmesan cheese
Sea salt and freshly ground pepper
2 links sweet Italian sausage (about 5 ounces), casings removed
1 teaspoon fennel seeds
1 teaspoon finely chopped fresh rosemary
¼ teaspoon red pepper flakes, plus more for serving
1 ball pizza dough (page 16), thawed if frozen
About 4 ounces fresh mozzarella cheese, torn into bite-size pieces

Preheat the oven to 550°F.

Bring a large pot of salted water to a boil. Add the broccoli rabe, stir, and cook until the water returns to a boil, the rabe is bright green, and the stems are barely tender. Drain and run under cold water to stop the cooking process. Let cool and then squeeze to remove any excess liquid. Separate out a handful of florets and set aside to use as topping. Roughly chop the remaining rabe.

continued

continued

Transfer the chopped rabe to a food processor and add the nuts, 4 tablespoons of the oil, and ½ cup of the Parmesan. Blitz until you have a relatively smooth mixture, adding more oil as needed a tablespoon or so at a time. Season with salt and pepper. Taste and tweak the seasoning as needed.

In a medium skillet, heat the remaining 2 tablespoons oil over medium-high heat. Add the sausage, reduce the heat to medium, and cook, using a wooden spoon to break it up. Add the fennel seeds, rosemary, and pepper flakes and cook until the meat is browned all the way through, about 8 minutes total. Taste for seasoning and fiddle as needed.

Shape the pizza crust as directed in the master recipe. Smear the rabe pesto evenly over the crust using the back of a spoon. Scatter the mozzarella evenly over the crust. Add the sausage and reserved rabe florets, and sprinkle with the remaining ½ cup Parmesan and a bit more pepper flakes, if you like.

Transfer the pizza to the oven and bake until the crust is nicely browned and the cheese has melted, 6 to 10 minutes.

It's a little scary to think about how many bowls of broccoli rabe and sausage pasta I've made over the years (with a bit of white wine, pepper flakes, rosemary, and a good hunk of butter, it's as comforting as a hug after a rough day).

SAUTÉED ZUCCHINI, BACON, FRESH BASIL, AND MOZZARELLA

I am a complete and utter hypocrite when it comes to animals. I love them like a crazy lady, but yet I eat them. It's a character flaw I can't reconcile and, frankly, don't like to dwell on. Especially when it comes to pigs, because of all the animals I enjoy eating, the pig is probably my favorite in terms of deliciousness and versatility. Prosciutto, pancetta, guanciale (cured pork jowl), bacon, butt, you name it . . . I love it all. But this love is tempered by quality—meaning I don't eat just any pork, because it isn't all worth eating. Especially bacon. Some is lightly smoked, thick-cut, and meaty. That's the kind of bacon I like and the kind that seems to make anything taste good. It's also the kind you want when you're putting such a small amount on a pizza— it needs to be thick enough to have some bite, a little smoky, and not too salty so that the sweet zucchini, minty basil, and milky mozzarella don't get overwhelmed.

1 to 2 tablespoons extra virgin olive oil
2 slices thick-cut bacon, cut into ¼-inch pieces
1 medium zucchini, cut into ¼-inch rounds
Sea salt and freshly ground pepper
1 ball pizza dough (page 16), thawed if frozen
About 3 ounces fresh mozzarella cheese, torn into bite-size pieces
Handful of fresh basil leaves

Preheat the oven to 550°F.

In a medium skillet, heat 1 tablespoon of the oil over medium-high heat. Add the bacon, reduce the heat to medium, and cook, stirring occasionally, until the bacon has rendered its fat and is nicely colored but not crisp, 6 to 8 minutes. Use a slotted spoon to transfer the bacon to a small bowl along with a tablespoon or so of the rendered fat (do not blot the bacon on paper towels). Reserve the bacon fat in the skillet.

Use the bacon fat in the skillet to cook the zucchini, adding the remaining 1 tablespoon olive oil if necessary, and return to medium heat. Add the zucchini, sprinkle with salt and pepper, and cook until the squash is tender and beginning to brown in places, about 10 minutes. Remove from the heat.

Shape the pizza crust as directed in the master recipe. Brush the surface of the crust with the bacon fat in the bowl, leaving about a 1-inch border all around. Scatter the mozzarella over the crust along with the bacon, zucchini, and lots of torn basil leaves.

Transfer the pizza to the oven and bake until the crust is nicely browned and the cheese has melted, 6 to 10 minutes.

Of all the animals I enjoy eating, the pig is probably my favorite in terms of deliciousness and versatility. Prosciutto, pancetta, guanciale (cured pork jowl), bacon, butt, you name it . . . I love it all.

BALSAMIC-GLAZED RADICCHIO, FENNEL SAUSAGE, AND MOZZARELLA

Having a favorite pizza for me is kind of like having a favorite pet—I can't do it. I love them all in different ways. But this pizza is special somehow. It's soothing to make as well as to eat. Something about the claret-toned shreds of radicchio tangled up with the syrupy balsamic, the way the leaves wilt and weep in the vinegar, how it melts down into demure-looking little bundles, secretly screaming with flavor. It's a small step in the grand scheme of the pizza-making process, but for me this sort of sautéing and deglazing is a very meditative part of cooking; like stirring risotto or making lemon curd, the process is quiet but the outcome is full of energy.

2 to 3 tablespoons extra virgin olive oil

2 links sweet Italian sausage (about 5 ounces), casings removed

1 teaspoon fennel seeds, roughly crushed

1 head radicchio, very thinly sliced

Sea salt and freshly ground pepper

2 to 3 tablespoons good-quality balsamic vinegar, or to taste

1 ball pizza dough (page 16), thawed if frozen

About 3 ounces fresh mozzarella cheese, torn into bite-size pieces

¼ cup whole-milk ricotta cheese (optional)

Preheat the oven to 550°F.

In a medium saucepan or skillet, heat 2 tablespoons of the oil over medium-high heat. Add the sausage and fennel seeds, reduce the heat to medium, and cook, using a wooden spoon to break it up, until well browned, 5 to 7 minutes. Transfer to a small bowl.

Place the same skillet (with the fat from the sausage) over high heat to cook the radicchio, adding the remaining 1 tablespoon oil if necessary. When hot, add the radicchio and sprinkle with salt and pepper. Stir constantly (think of this as a stir-fry of sorts) until the thin leaves begin to wilt, about 3 minutes. Add 2 to 3 tablespoons of vinegar depending on how bright you want the flavor, and continue cooking over high heat until the liquid is nearly evaporated and just glazing the radicchio. Taste and season, if needed, with more vinegar, salt, and pepper.

Shape the pizza crust as directed in the master recipe. Scatter the mozzarella evenly over the crust. Top with the sausage and then spread tangles of the radicchio over everything. If you like, drop dollops of fresh ricotta randomly on top of the radicchio.

Transfer the pizza to the oven and bake until the crust is nicely browned and the cheese has melted, 6 to 10 minutes.

SPICY SAUSAGE AND WILD MUSHROOMS WITH RICOTTA

Ken is not a ricotta fan. In fact when I met him, he claimed he "didn't like cheese" in general. Admittedly he did eat it on pizza, but that didn't count, he assured me: It was mozzarella. Over the years he has grown into what I'd call a picky cheese eater but an adventurous one nonetheless. He won't eat everything I bring home, but he'll try anything and usually admit to liking some aspect of it. But not ricotta. Even buried deep between the tomato sauce and sheets of pasta, nestled covertly into the layers of a lasagna, he can sense the presence of this creamy interloper and will wonder out loud at the perceived value it's adding to the overall dish. That is until I snuck it on this pizza one night. Somewhere between the spicy sausage and loamy mushrooms, he failed to notice that what was binding all of it together was the milky, sweet smear of fresh ricotta. I'm only slightly ashamed to admit I have not made any effort to enlighten him to my deceit.

3 to 4 tablespoons extra virgin olive oil
2 links hot Italian sausage (about 5 ounces), casings removed
2 cups quartered mixed mushrooms (cremini, button, shiitake, or other)
Leaves from 3 to 4 sprigs fresh thyme
Sea salt and freshly ground pepper
1 ball pizza dough (page 16), thawed if frozen
½ cup whole-milk ricotta cheese

Preheat the oven to 550°F.

In a large skillet, heat 2 tablespoons of the oil over medium-high heat. Add the sausage, reduce the heat to medium, and cook, using a wooden spoon to break it up, until well browned, 5 to 7 minutes. Transfer to a small bowl.

Place the same skillet (with the fat from the sausage) over medium-high heat to cook the mushrooms, adding the remaining 1 or 2 tablespoons oil if necessary. When hot, add the mushrooms and cook for a couple of minutes, stirring constantly. Reduce the heat to medium, add the thyme, sprinkle with salt and pepper, and cook until the mushrooms release their liquid, it evaporates, and they begin to caramelize on all sides, about 15 minutes. When the mushrooms are nicely colored, remove from the heat.

Shape the pizza crust as directed in the master recipe. Using the back of a spoon, smear the crust with half of the ricotta in an even layer, leaving about a 1-inch border all around. Sprinkle the sausage and mushrooms evenly over the ricotta and then dot with dollops of the remaining ricotta.

Transfer the pizza to the oven and bake until the crust is nicely browned and the cheese has softened, 6 to 10 minutes.

Somewhere between the spicy sausage and loamy mushrooms, he failed to notice that what was binding all of it together was the milky, sweet smear of fresh ricotta.

PROSCIUTTO, SWEET FIGS, AND MOZZARELLA WITH BALSAMIC

Is this a cliché? Probably, but there's a line in a song from one of my favorite singers, Lloyd Cole, that goes like this: "The reason it's a cliché is because it's true." Which is what this combination is, true to exactly what a pizza should be. When prosciutto is good, it can be as sweet as it is salty; when figs are ripe, they're sweet and sensual; fresh mozzarella should be milky, rich, and clean tasting; and decent balsamic is fruity and bright, lightening up the richness of the other ingredients. The combination may be a cliché, but with good reason.

1 ball pizza dough (page 16), thawed if frozen
About 3 ounces fresh mozzarella cheese, torn into bite-size pieces
4 to 6 slices prosciutto
4 fresh figs, quartered
Olive oil
Balsamic vinegar

Preheat the oven to 550°F.

Shape the pizza crust as directed in the master recipe.

Top the pizza with the mozzarella and prosciutto. Randomly scatter the figs over the prosciutto.

Transfer the pizza to the oven and bake until the crust is nicely browned and the cheese has melted, 6 to 10 minutes. To serve, drizzle the pie very lightly with olive oil and balsamic vinegar.

FRESH TOMATO SAUCE, MEATBALLS, AND CREMINI MUSHROOMS

I'm lucky to have a partner who not only likes to cook, but happens to be really good at it. Admittedly he has some signature dishes that he falls back on like we all do, the best in his repertoire being his Bolognese sauce (page 216). It's extraordinary. I've told him that if I ever end up in the hospital and it doesn't look good, he's to sneak in a container of his pasta Bolognese either as a last-ditch effort to save me or as my final meal. Truly, it's that good. However, when he makes it, for some reason he almost always ends up with an extra three-quarter pound of three different kinds of meat he doesn't need. Not enough to make another vat of Bolognese but exactly the right amount for me to make these meatballs, which bake in the oven while he labors over his bubbling pot on the stove. They're very fast, very easy and will ensure that after a life-affirming bowl of Bolognese on Sunday night, we'll have something meaty if not quite as memorable to look forward to on our pizza Monday night.

¼ pound ground beef
¼ pound ground pork
¼ pound ground veal
1 large egg
1 cup fresh breadcrumbs
Leaves from 2 sprigs fresh rosemary, finely chopped
½ teaspoon red pepper flakes, or more to taste
Sea salt and freshly ground pepper
2 tablespoons extra virgin olive oil
2 cups quartered cremini mushrooms
1 ball pizza dough (page 16), thawed if frozen
¼ cup Essential Pomodoro Sauce (page 25)
About 3 ounces fresh mozzarella cheese, torn into bite-size pieces
Handful of fresh basil leaves

Preheat the oven to 400°F.

In a large bowl, combine the beef, pork, veal, egg, breadcrumbs, rosemary, pepper flakes, and good sprinkle of salt and pepper. Use your hands to mix the ingredients together thoroughly, being careful not to overhandle the mixture or it will become tough. Pull off small fistfuls of the meat mixture, roll them into firm balls, and place them on a parchment paper–lined baking sheet. Roast the meatballs, turning once or twice so they color on all sides, until cooked through, 20 to 25 minutes. Remove from the oven and let cool. Increase the oven temperature to 550°F.

In a medium skillet, heat the oil over medium-high heat. Add the mushrooms and cook for a couple of minutes, stirring constantly. Reduce the heat to medium, sprinkle with salt and pepper, and cook until the mushrooms release their liquid, it evaporates, and they begin to caramelize on all sides, about 15 minutes. When the mushrooms are nicely colored, remove from the heat.

Shape the pizza crust as directed in the master recipe. Use the back of a wooden spoon to gently and evenly smear a thin layer of the sauce all over the crust, leaving about a 1-inch border all around. Scatter the mozzarella over the sauce. Using a sharp knife, slice or quarter the cooled meatballs and spread them over the cheese. Top everything with the caramelized mushrooms.

Transfer the pizza to the oven and bake until the crust is nicely browned and the cheese has melted, 6 to 10 minutes. To serve, toss the fresh basil leaves all over the top of the pizza.

I've told him that if I ever end up in the hospital and it doesn't look good, he's to sneak in a container of his pasta Bolognese either as a last-ditch effort to save me or as my final meal.

PICKLED RED ONIONS, ARUGULA, AND COPPA

Quick pickled onions are like preserved lemons—they're an easy way to add a bit of brightness to dishes and they're beautiful to boot. The pickling liquid is tinted purple and the onions are stained a vibrant, almost otherworldly peony pink hue. Sweet-sour onions with verdant arugula and spiced coppa is admittedly bold, but there's subtlety in the mix of textures. The coppa (a kind of dry-cured pork shoulder not unlike prosciutto) becomes a bit leathery when it cooks, like a jerky, while the crispness of the salad and tenderness of the pickles all ricochet off one another in a very layered way. Save the extra onions in an airtight jar and scatter them on fish tacos, roasted pork sandwiches, or almost anything—they're one of those keepers you'll find a way to use even when it's not pizza night.

½ cup water
½ cup distilled white vinegar
2 tablespoons sugar
½ teaspoon sea salt
1 bay leaf, preferably fresh
1 dried red chile
1 red onion, thinly sliced
1 ball pizza dough (page 16), thawed if frozen
1 tablespoon extra virgin olive oil
About 3 ounces fresh mozzarella cheese, torn into bite-size pieces
6 to 8 slices coppa, bresaola, or prosciutto
A few handfuls of baby arugula

Preheat the oven to 550°F.

In a small saucepan, bring the water to a boil. Add the vinegar, sugar, salt, bay leaf, and chile. Add the onions, reduce the heat, and let simmer for 1 minute. Remove the pan from the heat and let cool completely.

Shape the pizza crust as directed in the master recipe. Brush the crust with the oil, leaving about a 1-inch border all around. Scatter the mozzarella over the crust and lay the coppa over the cheese so the pieces overlap slightly.

Transfer the pizza to the oven and bake until the crust is nicely browned, 6 to 10 minutes. Meanwhile, in a medium bowl, toss the arugula with as many onions as you like, letting the pickling liquid serve as a light dressing for the greens. To serve, top the pizza with the arugula and onion salad.

SKIRT STEAK, CRESS, AND GORGONZOLA

Coming from California, I was raised to eat a salad as a main course for almost any meal. However, over the years I've learned that there is a cultural disparity between the two coasts when it comes to salad as a meal—especially when it's below 20°F outside. Which is how this pizza came to be. One really cold winter night, when it was far too chilly to try and put a salad on the table and call it dinner with a straight face, I took the ingredients I had and placed them on a crust. Resonant of a good bistro meal, this may not be remotely conventional, but it is hearty and a bit different. If you don't like Gorgonzola but are enchanted by the rest, you can go in a very different, albeit still French-inspired, direction and use Brie or even Camembert, both of which will melt nicely. A good fresh goat cheese is another lovely option; soft, milky puddles with lemony undertones are a good foil to the peppery cress.

About ½ pound skirt steak
Sea salt and freshly ground pepper
2 tablespoons extra virgin olive oil
1 ball pizza dough (page 16), thawed if frozen
8 to 12 cherry tomatoes, halved
About 3 ounces Gorgonzola or other good-quality blue cheese
1 bunch watercress (a few good handfuls)

Preheat the oven to 550°F.

Pat the steak dry with paper towels and sprinkle generously with salt and pepper. Put a cast iron skillet over high heat and add 1 tablespoon of the oil. When the oil is hot, add the steak and cook, turning once, until nicely seared on the outside and rare to medium-rare on the inside, about 5 minutes total. Remove from the pan and let rest. Reserve the pan, juices and all.

Shape the pizza crust as directed in the master recipe. Brush the crust with the remaining 1 tablespoon oil, leaving about a 1-inch border all around. Spread the tomatoes over the crust and dot with the Gorgonzola. Slice the steak into thin pieces and scatter them over the face of the pie.

Transfer the pizza to the oven and bake until the crust is nicely browned, the tomatoes have softened, and the cheese has melted, 6 to 10 minutes.

Meanwhile, heat the pan used for the steak over high heat. Add the cress, toss to coat in the remaining juices, and barely wilt, less than a minute.

To serve, use tongs to remove the cress from the pan, shake off any excess liquid, and drape the greens over the pizza.

BACON WITH ASPARAGUS RIBBONS

People tend to have strong feelings about asparagus. Growing up we didn't eat it very often because my dad didn't care for it; happily it's grown on him. However, he only really likes the pencil-thin variety, spears that I find are almost too delicate to bother cooking at all. Which is how this approach came to be. Finding the really thin kind of asparagus isn't always that easy, even in high season. To turn thicker spears into something more approachable for those who only want that tender hint of asparagus, I use a vegetable peeler to make gossamer-thin ribbons that curl up and mingle together in a grassy tangle when added to the pizza. I like to add the asparagus right at the end of the cooking time so it warms but doesn't totally wilt; if you prefer your asparagus more well done, you can of course add it at any point in the cooking process.

2 tablespoons extra virgin olive oil
2 slices thick-cut bacon, cut into ½-inch-wide
   pieces
3 to 4 medium thick asparagus spears, trimmed
Grated zest and juice of ½ lemon
Sea salt and freshly ground pepper
1 ball pizza dough (page 16), thawed if frozen
About 3 ounces fresh mozzarella cheese, torn into
   bite-size pieces
¼ cup freshly grated Parmesan cheese

Preheat the oven to 550°F.

In a medium skillet, heat 1 tablespoon of the oil over medium-high heat. Add the bacon, reduce the heat to medium, and cook, stirring occasionally, until the bacon is done but not crisp, 6 to 8 minutes. Reserve the bacon fat.

Meanwhile, using a vegetable peeler, slide the peeler down the asparagus spears lengthwise to create long, thin ribbons. Start on one side and peel around the spear—you won't be able to get all the way through the core of the spear, but that's okay. Put the ribbons in a bowl. Drizzle with the remaining 1 tablespoon oil and the lemon juice, sprinkle with the zest, and season with salt and pepper.

Shape the pizza crust as directed in the master recipe. Brush the surface of the crust with some of the bacon fat, leaving about a 1-inch border all around. Scatter the mozzarella over the crust, followed by the bacon.

Transfer the pizza to the oven and bake until the crust is nicely browned and the cheese has melted, 6 to 10 minutes. About 2 minutes before the pizza is done, pull it out and drape the asparagus ribbons over the top of the pie and sprinkle with the Parmesan. Return the pizza to the oven to warm and gently wilt the asparagus and barely melt the Parmesan before serving.

PANCETTA AND SHAVED BRUSSELS SPROUTS WITH TALEGGIO

We have a Thanksgiving dish we make every year that I adore. We fry pancetta until it's almost crisp, then add shaved Brussels spouts and cook them quickly in the fat—until they just turn bright green and start to become tender. Then we add a dash of sherry vinegar and scatter a good handful of maple-glazed pecans (see page 71) on top. It's one of those side dishes that I always mean to make more often, say on a random winter Sunday. But it never seems to happen; somehow the status of this side dish is reserved for just that one special day a year. I have, however, been unable to resist hijacking the notion of this combination for a fabulous pizza. With some creamy, tangy, almost fruity Taleggio added to the mix, it's a winter treat on a cold evening. Come to think of it, adding a handful of the salty-sweet pecans would be delicious, a pizza worthy of Thanksgiving if one were so inclined.

1 to 2 tablespoons extra virgin olive oil
¼ pound pancetta, cut into ¼-inch pieces
8 to 10 Brussels sprouts, trimmed
½ teaspoon sherry vinegar (or to taste)
Sea salt and freshly ground pepper
1 ball pizza dough (page 16), thawed if frozen
About 3 ounces Taleggio cheese

Preheat the oven to 550°F.

In a medium skillet, heat 1 tablespoon of the oil over medium-high heat. Add the pancetta and cook, stirring occasionally, until they firm up and just begin to color on the edges, 5 to 7 minutes. Using a slotted spoon, transfer the pancetta to a small bowl (don't feel compelled to blot them on paper towels—you want some fat to pool in the bowl for the crust).

Meanwhile, cut the sprouts into thin wedges (eighths is what I aim for).

Place the same skillet (with the fat from the pancetta) over medium-high heat to cook the sprouts, adding the remaining 1 tablespoon olive oil if necessary. When hot, add the sprouts and cook, stirring constantly, until just bright green, 1 to 2 minutes. Add the vinegar, increase the heat to high, and cook for another minute or until the liquid has evaporated. Remove from the heat and season with salt and pepper.

Shape the pizza crust as directed in the master recipe. Brush the crust with some of the fat that's dripped off the pancetta, leaving about a 1-inch border all around. Drop pieces of Taleggio randomly but evenly over the surface of the dough. Scatter the pancetta on top. Spread the sprouts over everything.

Transfer the pizza to the oven and bake until the crust is nicely browned, the cheese has melted, and the sprouts are beginning to color on the edges, 6 to 10 minutes. To serve, sprinkle with freshly ground pepper.

MARINATED GIGANTE BEANS AND SWEET SAUSAGE

I first had marinated gigante beans from Murray's Cheese Shop in downtown New York; they were marinated in olive oil and flavored with a slew of other herbs and aromatics. Wanting to re-create those creamy, tangy, garlicky beans at home, I started playing around with what I had in the house one summer afternoon. Lacking roasted red peppers, I used pepperoncini. I guessed at the rest. A dash of this and sprinkle of that until I had a mixture that seemed close to what I'd tasted and enjoyed. I put the beans and everything else in a jar, closed it tight, and let it sit for an hour or so. Happily it came surprisingly close to what I was hoping for, and we had my version of Marinated Gigante Beans (page 162) with our cocktails on the patio that night. I kept making these beans as a last-minute snack when we found ourselves with unexpected guests—just setting the jar out on the table with a stash of toothpicks for spearing. Then one day, searching the fridge for a way to spice up dinner, I spied the jar and decided to try them on a pizza. Sausage and beans like each other, so why not? Why not, indeed.

1 tablespoon extra virgin olive oil
2 links sweet Italian sausage (about 5 ounces), casings removed
1 teaspoon fennel seeds, roughly crushed
¼ teaspoon red pepper flakes (or to taste)
1 ball pizza dough (page 16), thawed if frozen
1 Roma tomato, very thinly sliced
About 3 ounces fresh mozzarella cheese, torn into bite-size pieces
About 1 cup Marinated Gigante Beans (page 162)

Preheat the oven to 550°F.

In a medium skillet, heat the oil over medium-high heat. When the oil is hot, add the sausage, fennel seeds, and pepper flakes and cook, using a wooden spoon to break up any clumps, until nicely browned all over, 8 to 10 minutes. Remove from the heat and use a slotted spoon to drain the sausage from the fat. Discard the fat.

Shape the pizza crust as directed in the master recipe. Lay the tomato slices evenly over the dough and top with the mozzarella and sausage.

Transfer the pizza to the oven and bake until the crust is nicely browned and the cheese has melted, 6 to 10 minutes.

To serve, spoon as much of the beans over the pizza as you like, being careful not to let too much of the marinade get on the crust or it can become soggy.

PEACHES, BRESAOLA, AND BURRATA

Stone fruit, cured beef, and fresh cheese. This may not sound like a good idea when you break it down that way, but it's really just a riff on the classic Italian combination of fruit—usually melon—and prosciutto. Bresaola, thinly sliced cured beef, replaces the pork, and peaches step in for the cantaloupe. If you're even a bit hesitant, start by wrapping a slice of ripe peach in a piece of bresaola first then taste it. Follow that bite with a spoonful of milky burrata. Then close your eyes and drift off for a minute: You're enjoying a picnic lunch overlooking a vineyard or an orchard. Bread torn in pieces for lack of a knife; cold, dry pink wine in plastic cups sitting in for proper stemmed glasses; and everything bought fresh that morning at an open market somewhere beautiful and far away or even at the farmers' market down the block. No matter, the taste is transporting.

1 ball pizza dough (page 16), thawed if frozen
1 tablespoon extra virgin olive oil
1 peach, thinly sliced
6 to 8 slices bresaola, whole or torn as desired
1 medium ball burrata
A few fresh basil leaves, torn

Preheat the oven to 550°F.

Shape the pizza crust as directed in the master recipe. Brush the crust evenly with the oil, leaving about a 1-inch border all around. Lay the peach slices over the dough in any fashion you like. Drape the bresaola over the peaches.

Transfer the pizza to the oven and bake until the crust is golden brown, the peaches have softened and begun to color slightly, and the bresaola is barely crisp, 6 to 10 minutes. To serve, add dollops of burrata randomly over the pizza and scatter the basil evenly over all.

continued

PAWLET WITH PANCETTA AND FRISÉE SALAD

Cheese is obviously a key ingredient in pizza, and while I'm guilty of falling back on the most traditional choices again and again, I've tried to explore and discover other cheeses that work well when melted or shaved, to keep things interesting. Over the last year or so, I've learned a lot about cheese in this quest—largely thanks to two dear friends. One of these women, cheese expert Liz Thorpe, taught me that European cheeses are identified by type (Brie, Gruyère, and so on) and the American artisanal cheeses are identified by producer name. Information I'm sure I should have garnered years ago, this knowledge has made my foray into understanding cheese incredibly easier and more rewarding (I'm not nearly as intimidated by the cheesemonger these days). My other pal, Angela Miller, goat farmer and owner of Consider Bardwell cheese company, is responsible for introducing me to one of my favorite cheeses: Pawlet, a creamy Italian-style toma *handmade on her farm in Vermont. Pawlet is a wonderful melter with just enough tang to stand up to the rich, smokiness of pancetta and a very bright French-style frisée salad. If you can't find Pawlet, Fontina will work nicely.*

4 tablespoons extra virgin olive oil
¼ pound pancetta, cut into ¼-inch pieces
1 shallot, finely chopped
2 tablespoons sherry vinegar (or to taste)
1 tablespoon Dijon mustard
Sea salt and freshly ground pepper
1 ball pizza dough (page 16), thawed if frozen
About 3 ounces Pawlet or Fontina cheese, cut into thin slices
½ head frisée

Preheat the oven to 550°F.

In a medium skillet, heat 1 tablespoon of the oil over medium-high heat. Add the pancetta, reduce the heat to medium, and cook, stirring occasionally, until just colored and crisping on the edges. Use a slotted spoon to transfer the pancetta to a small bowl and set aside. Reserve the fat from the pan.

In a small jar or other lidded container, combine the remaining 3 tablespoons oil, the shallot, vinegar, mustard, and some salt and pepper. Shake vigorously to emulsify. Taste and season a bit more if needed.

continued

continued

Shape the pizza crust as directed in the master recipe. Brush the crust with a thin layer of the reserved pancetta fat. Lay the cheese randomly but evenly over the crust. Scatter the reserved pancetta over the cheese.

Transfer the pizza to the oven and bake until the crust is nicely browned and the cheese has melted, 6 to 10 minutes.

Meanwhile, toss the frisée in a bowl with enough dressing to coat the leaves well. Remove the pizza from the oven and place the salad over the entire face of the pie. To serve, season with more pepper.

Cheese is obviously a key ingredient in pizza, and while I'm guilty of falling back on the most traditional choices again and again, I've tried to explore and discover other cheeses that work well when melted or shaved, to keep things interesting.

PERSIMMON, RICOTTA, AND CHORIZO

I didn't know what a persimmon was until I was about 16. At that point I was already interested in cooking and was captivated by the Sunday food column in the Los Angeles Times Magazine. *One issue featured a recipe for persimmon pudding—a holiday dessert attributed to none other than Nancy Reagan. It was in fact called Nancy Reagan's Persimmon Pudding. Raised in a very liberal California household, I was naturally skeptical of anything Reagan. That, coupled with the fact that the woman I watched on the news at night in the pretty dresses with matching hats and shoes didn't look like the type who cooked a lot, left me suspicious. But my suspicion was overcome by my fascination with this thing called a persimmon. It was exotic looking, and its taste was yet to be tried. How could I walk away? So my mom and I made the pudding. It was a dense, dark, moist fruitcake served with a brandy cream sauce, and it was undeniably good. But the persimmon flavor—that sweet, honeyed, dewy taste that I'd only just been introduced to—was subdued, overwhelmed by the sugar and the boozy cream sauce. I may have been disappointed (I don't remember) but I had discovered the persimmon and for that I'll always be thankful. There are different kinds of persimmons. Here I use the fuyu, which can be sliced thinly like a peach or a tomato. You can use the softer, heartshaped hachiya, which are pulpier when ripe, but just know they won't slice as easily; it'll be more of a smear or dollop.*

1 tablespoon extra virgin olive oil
1 link fresh chorizo sausage (about 2 to 3 ounces), casing removed
1 ball pizza dough (page 16), thawed if frozen
About 3 ounces fresh mozzarella cheese, torn into bite-size pieces
1 ripe fuyu persimmon, halved and thinly sliced
¼ cup whole-milk ricotta cheese
Sea salt

Preheat the oven to 550°F.

In a medium skillet, heat the oil over medium-high heat. Add the chorizo, reduce the heat to medium, and cook, stirring occasionally and using a wooden spoon or fork to break up any clumps, until done. Transfer the chorizo to a small bowl. Reserve the cooking fat.

Shape the pizza crust as directed in the master recipe. Brush the crust with the thinnest layer of spicy fat from the chorizo pan. Scatter the mozzarella over the crust, layer the persimmon slices over the cheese, and sprinkle with the chorizo.

Transfer the pizza to the oven and bake until the crust is nicely browned and the cheese has melted, 6 to 10 minutes. To serve, dot the pizza with dollops of the ricotta and season lightly with salt.

SOPPRESSATA, SAUTÉED KALE, OLIVE OIL, AND FLAKE SALT

This pizza is as much about texture as it is taste. When soppressata is thinly sliced, it crisps up and curls on the edges and is a perfect complement to similarly cut tender ribbons of kale. When I don't have kale in the house, I use broccoli rabe (small cooked portions of which I tend to have in the freezer as we eat so much of it); the rabe is lovely but it's a tad bitter, so it offers up even more of a contrast in flavor to the sweet salami. I don't feel the need for anything else here, but if you ask my better half, he will say that a thinly sliced Roma tomato underneath the other toppings won't go awry.

2 tablespoons extra virgin olive oil
½ bunch kale, trimmed, ribs removed, and torn into ribbons
Sea salt and freshly ground pepper
1 ball pizza dough (page 16), thawed if frozen
About 3 ounces fresh mozzarella cheese, torn into bite-size pieces
6 to 8 thin slices sweet soppressata
Maldon or other flake salt

Preheat the oven to 550°F.

In a large sauté pan, heat the oil over medium-high heat. When the oil is hot, add the kale, sprinkle with a bit of salt and pepper, and cook, stirring constantly, until the leaves have just wilted. Remove from the heat and let cool. Squeeze to remove any excess liquid, if needed.

Shape the pizza crust as directed in the master recipe. Top with the mozzarella. Lay the soppressata over the cheese in an even layer and then scatter the kale over everything.

Transfer the pizza to the oven and bake until the crust is nicely browned, the cheese has melted, and the kale is crisp, 6 to 10 minutes. To serve, sprinkle lightly with Maldon salt.

PORCHETTA-STYLE PORK WITH FENNEL AND ASIAGO

A few years ago in Umbria, we wandered into a small town market to pick up some provisions. As I've since learned is commonplace in Italy, the market was lined not only with stalls of farmers selling impossibly pungent cheeses, glorious fruits and vegetables of every imaginable shape, color, and size, and charcuterie varied enough to make a carnivore's head spin, but also with a slew of trucks dedicated to porchetta sandwiches. Traditionally made from a whole roasted pig, porchetta is an intensely spiced regional delicacy, usually flavored with some combination of rosemary, fennel, garlic, and pepper. As we meandered down the wiggly street, we noticed that each truck had a long line of customers patiently waiting as the vendor sliced the pale, highly spiced meat, laid it on the scale, and then added in a shard of crispy pork skin for good measure. Clearly each local was partial to a specific porchetta purveyor and made weekly sojourns to their favorite for rations. Not knowing one from the other, we chose a line, not the longest but not the shortest, and bought what seemed like a reasonable amount. Once home, we all began tearing off small pieces of meat and crispy skin before it made its way to a plate. Suddenly our reasonable amount of pork for lunch was gone, along with any chance of adding some to a pizza that night. The lesson here was evident: When buying porchetta in Italy, buy more than you think is reasonable and don't be shy or you'll miss out.

2 tablespoons extra virgin olive oil
1 bulb fennel, trimmed and very thinly sliced
Sea salt
1 ball pizza dough (page 16), thawed if frozen
About 1 cup shredded Porchetta-Style Pulled Pork (page 211)
¼ cup Caramelized Onion Jam (page 27), made with onions or leeks
About 2 ounces Asiago cheese, grated
Freshly ground pepper

Preheat the oven to 550°F.

In a large skillet, heat the oil over medium-high heat. When the oil is hot, add the fennel, sprinkle with salt, and reduce the heat to medium. Cook the fennel, stirring occasionally, until it's wilted and beginning to caramelize, about 10 minutes. If the pan gets too dry, add a couple tablespoons of water to keep the fennel from burning and to help it cook down. When the fennel is a lovely golden tangle and the pan is dry, remove from the heat.

Shape the pizza crust as directed in the master recipe. If you're feeling decadent and have saved some of the fatty juices from the pork, brush them over the crust. If not, simply smear the onion jam over the dough, leaving a 1-inch border all around. Sprinkle half of the Asiago over the jam, drape the fennel over the cheese, scatter the pork, and sprinkle with the remaining cheese. Transfer the pizza to the oven and bake until the crust is nicely browned, 6 to 10 minutes.

SOPPRESSATA AND FRESH RED ONION

There are a few things you'll almost always find in my fridge: a hunk of Parmesan and a few lingering rinds, various other cheese nubs, small plastic tubs of different kinds of olives, and always a bit of prosciutto or sweet soppressata. A slice or two fills out an easy weekend lunch, but it also provides perfect fodder for a last-minute pizza dinner. When we're both knackered and almost ready to give in to going out, this combination smacks some homemade sense into our lazy bones and says, "Seriously? You can't slice up some soppressata and a bit of onion? Nobody is that tired . . . " True, it's just too easy and satisfying in its utter simplicity not to acquiesce. It would take longer to agree on a restaurant or dig up a menu and order than it does to get this pizza in the oven. So we give in, exhausted but also sated.

1 ball pizza dough (page 16), thawed if frozen
¼ cup Essential Pomodoro Sauce (page 25)
About 3 ounces fresh mozzarella cheese, torn into bite-size pieces
6 to 8 thin slices sweet soppressata, cut into ½-inch strips
½ small red onion, thinly sliced

Preheat the oven to 550°F. Shape the pizza crust as directed in the master recipe.

Gently smear the crust with the sauce, leaving about a 1-inch border all around. Top the sauce with the mozzarella, then scatter the soppressata and red onion over the entire pie.

Transfer the pizza to the oven and bake until the crust is nicely browned, the cheese has melted, and the soppressata and onions begin to color on the edges, 6 to 10 minutes.

This combination smacks some homemade sense into our lazy bones and says, "Seriously? You can't slice up some soppressata and a bit of onion? Nobody is that tired . . . "

POULTRY *and* SEAFOOD PIZZAS

I started putting chicken on pizza after eating one very memorable wood oven–baked pie at a little pizzeria in Milford, Connecticut (story to follow, stay tuned). I began using anchovies and sardines on pizza when I was home alone, hankering for a fix of those wonderfully briny, oil-cured fish that I just can't convince Ken to embrace. And I first put shellfish on pizza as a way to sneak Old Bay into our repertoire more frequently (a guilty secret pleasure, that all-American spice mix that reminds me of summer no matter what the calendar says). None of this came as naturally to me as prosciutto or Parmesan, but for a cook, that's not a bad thing.

It's true, of all the pizzas I make, the ones with poultry and seafood on them are the most intuitively unfamiliar to me. Meaning, they stretch me more as a cook and force me to be thoughtful in how I put things together. I have friends who are chefs and who radiate creativity in the kitchen. Thai fish sauce on grapefruit? That sounds like a good idea. Pink peppercorns in a meringue? But of course! I'm not like that. I err on the traditional, tried-and-true side of flavor combinations. But I like to push myself to try new things, and pizza is a place where I'm very comfortable exploring. (However, I also believe that hundreds and hundreds of years of regional cooking have produced certain reliably delicious flavor combinations, ones that might not be traditional on pizza but are perfectly suited for it.) To nudge my creative spirit along, it helps me to think of a pizza crust like any other starch—what ingredients or flavors work well together on a nest of pappardelle, in a bowl of risotto, or on a bed of couscous? Chances are good the same things will translate to a crust.

Chicken especially is a fantastic pizza topping because like chicken in almost any form, it needs other flavors to give it shape. When you roast a chicken, you need at minimum to add olive oil, salt, and pepper to bring out its sweet, chicken-y taste. But you're even better off with some tarragon, rosemary, or thyme, maybe some garlic or lemon in the mix. Chicken on a pizza is the same: Pair it with herbs, vegetables, or even other meats and you'll find it comes to life. Duck is a little different. It has a stronger, gamier flavor to begin with, so I tend to keep the flavor combinations subtle—I stay in the world I know and tend toward creamy beans, earthy mushrooms, or nutty brown onions.

Seafood on pizza can be challenging. First, there's the belief that seafood and cheese don't work together (not unilaterally true). Then there's the polarizing anchovy—for everyone who finds their bliss in a bite of that salty, skeletal little fish, there seem to be 10 who can't abide them. But there's a lot to be said for a spiced shrimp pie or a creamy clam pizza. Using seafood on pizzas just takes a little bit more thought to be sure you're mixing and matching flavors and textures that play well together.

Every cook has dishes that require them to work a bit harder; dinners that can't necessarily be whipped up with the phone in one hand and a knife in the other. Some of my best pizzas have come about because I had to think a bit longer, had to noodle on what ingredients would work well together. Poultry and seafood both force me to ponder my pairings . . . and that's not a bad thing.

ANCHOVY, FRESH CHILE, CAPERS, AND OREGANO

Pastis is a New York City landmark at this point—one of the first restaurants to gentrify the Meatpacking District. It is also, by virtue of our having lived in the neighborhood since before gentrification, my take-out joint. We don't order in often, but when we do, we are lucky enough to have a reliably good brasserie bring food to our front door. When I call to order, I'm pretty sure the very sweet woman on the end of the line rolls her eyes, as we always order exactly the same thing. Cheddar cheeseburger medium and a tuna Niçoise salad medium-rare. Every time. We share both, but the best part of the salad is all mine: the marinated white anchovies they lay across the top. On a good night, I get four, on an okay night only two, and when they forget entirely, well, it's just not the same salad and my night just took a turn for the worse. These anchovies are delicious— and they're what you want to buy if you're going to make this pizza. Nothing like the small, brown, highly salted ones you're used to getting on pizza (which have their place, mind you), the Spanish call these silvery fish boquerones, and they're soft, briny, meaty, tender and as good on this pizza as they are on Pastis's Niçoise salad. Or nearly.

6 marinated white anchovy fillets, halved lengthwise
½ small fresh red chile, seeded and thinly sliced
1 tablespoon small capers (or to taste)
2 tablespoons extra virgin olive oil
Grated zest and juice of ½ lemon
1 ball pizza dough (page 16), thawed if frozen
¼ cup Essential Pomodoro Sauce (page 25)
About 3 ounces fresh mozzarella cheese, torn into bite-size pieces
Leaves from 2 to 3 sprigs fresh oregano
Freshly ground pepper

Preheat the oven to 550°F.

In a medium bowl, stir together the anchovies, chile, capers, oil, lemon zest, and lemon juice. Let sit at room temperature to marinate for about 10 minutes.

Shape the pizza crust according to the master recipe. Use the back of a spoon to smear the sauce over the crust, leaving about a 1-inch border all around. Scatter the mozzarella over the sauce. Scoop out the solids from the anchovy mixture and spoon evenly over the crust (set the remaining marinade aside). Scatter the oregano over everything.

Transfer the pizza to the oven and bake until the crust is nicely browned and the cheese has melted, 6 to 10 minutes. To serve, drizzle some of the reserved marinade over the pizza and sprinkle with black pepper.

ANCHOVY, OLIVE, FRESH TOMATO, AND MOZZARELLA

Pan con tomate, *that simple yet sublime Spanish tapas, was part of the inspiration for this pizza. That and the fact that Ken will only eat anchovies if he doesn't see them or know they're there, like in a dressing or, in this case, mashed up in a smear of grated fresh tomato. By grating the tomato until it's pulpy, then adding and mashing in the anchovies, the flavor is integrated but not overpowering. It's potent enough for those who love anchovies and subtle enough for those who say they don't. With black olives and oregano as well, this is an assertively flavored pizza, one that echoes Spain but also hints at Provence—a bit of a Mediterranean melting pot.*

1 large tomato
2 to 3 oil-packed anchovy fillets
Sea salt and freshly ground pepper
1 ball pizza dough (page 16), thawed if frozen
About 3 ounces fresh mozzarella cheese, torn into bite-size pieces
Handful of Kalamata or Niçoise olives, pitted and halved
Leaves from 2 or 3 sprigs fresh oregano

Preheat the oven to 550°F.

Set a box grater inside a medium bowl (or a bowl large enough to hold it) and grate the tomato using the side with the largest teeth. You should end up with a slightly thick, juicy, pulpy mixture. Grate as much of the tomato as possible, until all that's left is the remnant of some skin (discard this last bit).

Add the anchovies to the grated tomato and, using a fork, mash them up until they're relatively well blended. Taste the mixture and decide if you need to add some salt—the anchovies are pretty salty so you may not. Sprinkle with a bit of pepper.

Shape the pizza crust as directed in the master recipe. Use the back of a spoon to lightly smear the tomato-anchovy mixture over the crust, leaving about a 1-inch border all around. Dot the tomato mixture with the mozzarella and olives.

Transfer the pizza to the oven and bake until the crust is nicely browned and the cheese has melted, 6 to 10 minutes. To serve, scatter the fresh oregano over the pizza.

ROAST CHICKEN WITH FENNEL AND ONION JAM

Long before I was cooking professionally, I found myself walking up Sixth Avenue one night with a friend, bracing ourselves against that first bitterly cold New York City wind (you know, the one that cuts through the far-too-light jacket you left home with that morning and reminds you that the long, dark days are just beginning?) and lamenting what to make for dinner. I was headed to Jefferson Market (sadly, it's no longer there) and had only a couple more blocks to figure out my plan when she said, "Why not just make a roast chicken?" The tone in her voice was so casual; she tossed off this bold suggestion with such relaxed assurance that I was taken aback. A whole chicken? It seemed so formal, so complete. Even for someone who regularly cooked what I imagined to be serious food (i.e., dishes with French and Italian names that required fresh herbs, bottles of wine, and an afternoon to cook), I'd never taken on a whole bird. But my life was about to change. "Rub some olive oil on it, sprinkle it with salt and pepper, and shove some herbs under the skin or a lemon slice. It'll be great," she said very convincingly. And, as I learned that night, a roast chicken is probably one of the simplest, most foolproof dinners you can make. My recipe is insanely easy and utterly reliable (see page 213), but if you don't have the time or inclination to take it on for whatever reason, add a couple of extra thighs or a breast to the baking sheet or grill next time you make chicken.

2 tablespoons extra virgin olive oil, plus more as needed

1 Vidalia or other sweet onion, thinly sliced

Sea salt and freshly ground pepper

1 fennel bulb, trimmed and thinly sliced, fronds reserved and chopped

About ¼ cup water

1 ball pizza dough (page 16), thawed if frozen

About 3 ounces fresh mozzarella cheese, torn into bite-size pieces

About ½ cup shredded cooked chicken, preferably home-roasted (page 213)

Preheat the oven to 550°F.

In a medium saucepan, heat the oil over medium-high heat. When the oil is hot, add the onion and sprinkle with salt and pepper. Reduce the heat to medium and cook, stirring occasionally, until the onion begins to soften, about 5 minutes.

Add the sliced fennel and a bit more oil if necessary, and sprinkle with more salt. Cook until the vegetables become very tender and begin to color, 10 to 12 minutes. When they just begin to brown on the edges, add the water, increase the heat to medium-high, and continue to cook until all the liquid has evaporated and both the onion and fennel are very tender and nicely colored, 15 minutes. Remove from the heat and set aside. (This will be more than you'll need for one pizza. You can freeze the leftovers.)

Shape the pizza crust as directed in the master recipe. Use the back of a spoon to gently smear the onion-fennel mixture over the crust, leaving about a 1-inch border all around. Scatter the mozzarella randomly over the crust, then top with shredded chicken.

Transfer the pizza to the oven and bake until the crust is nicely browned and the cheese has melted, 6 to 10 minutes. To serve, sprinkle the reserved fennel fronds over the pizza.

A whole chicken? It seemed so formal, so complete.
Even for someone who regularly cooked what I imagined to
be serious food (i.e., dishes with French and Italian names that
required fresh herbs, bottles of wine, and an afternoon to cook),
I'd never taken on a whole bird.

SHREDDED CHICKEN WITH SWEET CORN AND CHERRY TOMATOES

There are two ways to make this pizza work. One is in midsummer when fresh, sweet corn is abundant and cherry tomatoes are at their peak of ripeness. For this version (which is how the recipe is written), you can get away with barely cooking the corn and leaving the tomatoes totally untouched, and it will be fantastic. The other way (which is how those of us who don't live in California have to do it for most of the year) is to use frozen corn and grape tomatoes. Add the tomatoes to the pan along with the corn and let them cook down for a few minutes, giving their juices a chance to seep out and the flavors meld together. Yes, I admit, the first approach is beautiful and seasonal, like summer on a crust. But the other is still a really great dinner.

2 tablespoons extra virgin olive oil
½ small red onion, sliced
Sea salt and freshly ground pepper
1 ear of corn, kernels scraped off
1 ball pizza dough (page 16), thawed if frozen
2 to 3 ounces goat cheese
Handful or more of cherry tomatoes, halved
About ½ cup shredded cooked chicken, preferably home-roasted (page 213)

Preheat the oven to 550°F.

In a medium skillet, heat the oil over medium-high heat. Add the onion, reduce the heat to medium, sprinkle with salt, and cook, stirring occasionally, until soft and translucent, 8 to 10 minutes. Add the corn, increase the heat to high, and cook until the kernels turn bright yellow, about 2 minutes. Season with more salt, if needed, and pepper and remove from the heat.

Shape the pizza crust as directed in the master recipe. Spread the onion-corn mix evenly over the crust, leaving about a 1-inch border all around. Dot the top with small dollops of the goat cheese in a random but even fashion, then scatter the tomatoes and shredded chicken over everything.

Transfer the pizza to the oven and bake until the crust is nicely browned and the cheese has softened, 6 to 10 minutes.

DUCK CONFIT, CANNELLINI BEANS, AND CARAMELIZED ONIONS WITH ROSEMARY

If you haven't already guessed, this is my way of putting cassoulet on a pizza—or at least putting the flavors together in a way that echoes cassoulet. The funny thing about cassoulet (that rich French stew commonly made of beans, sausage, and duck) is that it used to be a peasant meal born of leftovers, but today duck leg confit is an extravagance. And while you can buy one at many good grocery stores, it's not cheap. So if you don't feel like spending the money, or if you can't find a duck leg confit in the butcher department, don't fret. Rub a couple of chicken thighs and/or drumsticks with olive oil, sprinkle them with salt and pepper, and bake them until nice and crisp. Dark meat chicken won't have the same intense gamey flavor as duck, but it works well and is definitely easier to come by and more affordable. Then all you have to do is have your crust and onion jam ready and waiting in the freezer, sear the duck leg and the sausage, open a can of beans, and grate some cheese. Do this all on a cold winter night when you have a hankering for a really good glass of red wine and a crackling fire—do it even if you don't have the good wine or the fireplace.

1 tablespoon extra virgin olive oil
1 duck leg confit
1 sweet Italian sausage link
1/4 cup Caramelized Onion Jam (page 27)
1 ball pizza dough (page 16), thawed if frozen
1 Roma tomato, thinly sliced
About 3 ounces fresh mozzarella cheese, torn into bite-size pieces
1/2 cup canned cannellini beans, drained and rinsed
Leaves from 1 to 2 sprigs fresh rosemary, finely chopped
1/4 cup freshly grated Parmesan cheese

Preheat the oven to 550°F.

In a medium saucepan, heat the oil over medium-low heat. When the oil is hot, place the duck leg skin-side down in the pan. Allow the duck to cook without turning, until the fat renders, the leg releases easily from the surface of the pan, and the skin has turned a deep, crispy, golden brown, at least 6 to 8 minutes. Turn the leg over and continue to cook until that side is well browned also. If there are still fatty spots on the top edge or sides of the leg, use tongs to hold the leg so that the uncooked areas come in contact with the pan and the fat renders and gets crisp. Remove from the heat and let cool. Drain all but 1 tablespoon of fat from the pan.

To the saucepan with the duck fat, add the sausage and sear over medium heat on all sides. Continue cooking until it's cooked through. Remove from the heat. Once cool, slice into disks.

When the duck is cool enough to handle, remove the meat and crispy skin from the bone. Shred the meat into bite-size pieces (save half for a second pizza).

Shape the pizza crust as directed in the master recipe. Use the back of a spoon to gently spread the caramelized onions over the crust, leaving about a 1-inch border all around. Lay the tomato on top, then add the sausage. Scatter the mozzarella, beans, and rosemary over everything. Scatter the duck meat, along with pieces of the crispy skin, over the pie and sprinkle with the Parmesan.

Transfer the pizza to the oven and bake until the crust is nicely browned and the cheese has melted, 6 to 10 minutes.

Do this all on a cold winter night when you have a hankering for a really good glass of red wine and a crackling fire—do it even if you don't have the good wine or the fireplace.

CHERRY PEPPERS, ONION, AND CHICKEN SAUSAGE

Before we had a cottage of our own, we used to rent places for a week or so each summer. For a few years we rented a mouse hole of a place in Chatham, Cape Cod, where cooking consisted of grilled fish, corn on the cob, and peach and tomato salads. Our happiest rental days were the ones spent on a small lake in Tuckertown, Rhode Island. We found the house online, and the first time we drove up we both gasped: The "cottage" was a beautiful house, not big by most American standards, but for two apartment dwellers, it was a palace. Cooking was a joy here, as the kitchen was far better appointed than what we had at home. But the rented-house-cooking-situation I remember most vividly was in New Hampshire. Desperate to get away, we booked a last-minute trip to a cottage on a lake somewhere in the wilds of the state. It took forever to get there, and upon arriving I found a book documenting the history of the lake. A young couple on their honeymoon had drowned in the early 1900s when an electrical storm struck their canoe. This was not what I'd hoped for. It rained much of the trip and the shower, which was outside, ran only cold water. We got lost on a hike our second day—having foolishly packed no water or food. After that misadventure we stayed close to our borrowed home, read mystery books, sat on the screened-in deck, and paddled around in the canoe when the sky was very, very clear. We also cooked, and one rainy night we made this pizza, the crust rolled out using an empty wine bottle.

2 tablespoons extra virgin olive oil
1 link fresh chicken sausage, casing removed
1 ball pizza dough (page 16), thawed if frozen
¼ cup Essential Pomodoro Sauce (page 25)
½ red onion, very thinly sliced
2 to 3 pickled cherry peppers, thinly sliced
About 3 ounces fresh mozzarella cheese, torn into bite-size pieces
Flake sea salt

Preheat the oven to 550°F.

In a medium skillet, heat the oil over high heat. When the oil is hot, reduce the heat to medium, add the sausage, and cook, stirring to break up any clumps. Continue to cook until the sausage is cooked through, about 8 minutes. Remove from the heat.

Shape the pizza crust as directed in the master recipe. Use the back of a spoon to smear the sauce evenly over the crust, leaving about a 1-inch border all around. Spread the onion over the sauce, add the cherry peppers and sausage, and dot with the mozzarella. Sprinkle with flake salt.

Transfer the pizza to the oven and bake until the crust is nicely browned and the cheese has melted, 6 to 10 minutes.

ANDOUILLE SAUSAGE, CHERRY TOMATOES, AND BABY SHRIMP

For reasons that should be obvious, we don't have pizza delivered very often. But every now and then, when it's just too late or we're just too tired, when Chinese doesn't sound appealing and we don't feel like wandering out, we order from Two Boots. I went to Two Boots at their original location in Alphabet City when I first moved to New York. I think my uncle had recommended it. This was before pizza had become a competitive cuisine among trendy restaurants, and they had an angle: fusion flavors from the two boots, Italy and Louisiana. It was a gimmick of sorts, but it was also good pizza. Now there's one a couple blocks away from our apartment, and it's still reliable. The crust is the same as it always was, and the delivery guys are fast. Of course I prefer making the pizza myself, but sometimes it's nice to have it brought to you in an insulated red pouch. So this is my homage to Two Boots. Because long before I had a life that allowed me to be home in time to cook most nights, and a job that meant I got to obsess over pizza, Two Boots kept us, at least partially, fed.

¼ cup Essential Pomodoro Sauce (page 25)
¼ teaspoon red pepper flakes (or to taste)
1 ball pizza dough (page 16), thawed if frozen
About 3 ounces fresh mozzarella cheese, torn into bite-size pieces
1 andouille sausage link, cut into ¼-inch slices
8 cherry or grape tomatoes, quartered
1 cup baby shrimp
Leaves from 2 to 3 sprigs fresh flat-leaf parsley
Freshly shaved Manchego cheese

Preheat the oven to 550°F.

In a small bowl, combine the sauce and pepper flakes. Taste and add more pepper flakes if necessary—you want a slightly spicy sauce here to complement the sweet tomatoes and shrimp.

Shape the pizza crust as directed in the master recipe. Use the back of a spoon to gently smear the sauce over the crust, leaving about a 1-inch border all around. Dot the sauce with the mozzarella. Evenly place the sausage slices over the cheese, then scatter the fresh tomatoes and shrimp over everything.

Transfer the pizza to the oven and bake until the crust is nicely browned and the cheese has melted, 6 to 10 minutes. To serve, sprinkle the parsley leaves and the Manchego over the pizza.

OLD BAY SHRIMP, PICKLED RED ONIONS, SWEET CORN, AND HEIRLOOM TOMATOES

Go ahead, mock me. Tease me. Make fun of the Old Bay . . . but I love it. I sprinkle Old Bay on roasted potatoes, on corn for the grill, I add a dash to my crab cakes, and even sprinkle it (with a bit of a heavy hand, I'm told) on popcorn. I just love the familiar seaside, summertime, celery salt-and-spice flavor that comes in that unmistakable little metal box. I even love the little metal box. Old Bay may be a culinary no-no to some, but it's the secret ingredient that makes this pizza special—that and the fact that you really can only make this when the corn is at its sweetest and the tomatoes are practically falling off the vine with ripeness. It's a seasonal pizza if there ever was one.

½ cup distilled white vinegar
½ cup water
2 tablespoons sugar
1 teaspoon red pepper flakes
½ teaspoon sea salt
1 large red onion, thinly sliced
½ pound medium shrimp, peeled and deveined
1 tablespoon extra virgin olive oil
2 tablespoons Old Bay seasoning
1 ball pizza dough (page 16), thawed if frozen
1 large or 2 small heirloom tomatoes, thinly sliced
1 ear of corn, kernels scraped off
About ½ cup queso fresco
A handful of fresh cilantro leaves

Preheat the oven to 550°F.

In a small saucepan, combine the vinegar, water, sugar, pepper flakes, and salt and bring to a boil. Add the onion, cover, and let brew for about 1 minute. Remove from the heat, transfer the onions and their liquid to an airtight container, and let cool.

Meanwhile, in a medium bowl, toss the shrimp with the oil and the Old Bay until evenly coated.

Shape the pizza crust as directed in the master recipe. Lay the tomato slices evenly over the surface. Sprinkle the corn over the tomatoes, top with the shrimp, and sprinkle with the queso fresco.

Transfer the pizza to the oven and bake until the crust is nicely browned and the shrimp are cooked through, 6 to 10 minutes. To serve, drape a few pickled red onions over the shrimp and scatter the cilantro over everything.

ROAST CHICKEN, BACON, GARLIC, AND PLUM TOMATOES

Ken grew up on Bleecker Street in Manhattan and I'm from Los Angeles—but a few years ago we moved up to Milford, Connecticut, for his job. For two urbanites, spending a year living in a smallish suburban town in an old house with a garden was a life-changer. We loved having a proper-size kitchen, so the entire time we lived there we didn't go out to eat even once—we cooked and grilled and cooked some more. Our landlord however did tell us about a pizzeria called Papa's just a mile up the road. He'd even left a menu stuck to the fridge for us. He said it was incredible. It turned out he was a part owner, so we were skeptical. We'd heard of course how famous pizza from New Haven is (a few miles north of Milford), but this was a small place in a little strip mall next to the hospital. Our knee-jerk reaction was pure pizza snobbery, but once we tried it we were quickly humbled. Papa's makes some of the best pizza in the world, or at least in my world, having mastered the crust, with great chew and just enough char to remind you you're eating brick-oven pizza. Today when we find ourselves passing through Milford to get the car serviced or on our way to somewhere north, we call and get pizza to go, often two. It's that good. This combo, which became one of our favorites, is called A 'Pizza Di Pietrini on their menu. And while I'm quite sure my recipe won't live up to theirs, if you can't get to Papa's, it's worth a try.

1 tablespoon extra virgin olive oil
2 slices thick-cut bacon, cut into 2-inch pieces
1 ball pizza dough (page 16), thawed if frozen
1 garlic clove, finely minced
About 3 ounces fresh mozzarella cheese, torn into bite-size pieces
1 Roma tomato, very thinly sliced
About ½ cup shredded cooked chicken, preferably home-roasted (page 213)
Leaves from 1 to 2 sprigs fresh basil, cut into very thin ribbons
Sea salt and freshly ground pepper

Preheat the oven to 550°F.

In a medium skillet, heat the oil over medium-high heat. Add the bacon, reduce the heat to medium, and cook, stirring frequently, until the bacon renders its fat and browns but doesn't become crisp. Use a slotted spoon and transfer the bacon to a small bowl. Reserve the bacon fat.

Shape the pizza crust as directed in the master recipe. Brush the crust lightly with the bacon fat, leaving about a 1-inch border all around. Sprinkle the garlic on top, scatter the cheese evenly around, and lay the tomato slices on top. Add the bacon and chicken to the pizza and finish with the basil ribbons.

Transfer the pizza to the oven and bake until the crust is nicely browned and the cheese has melted, 6 to 10 minutes. To serve, season with salt and pepper.

CHICKEN, BACON, AND PAPER-THIN APPLE SLICES

Living on the East Coast, I find that there are a few defining days in the year that remind me why I don't just pack up and move back to California. One is that first day when you actually feel spring—that bright too-blue morning when you realize you can go out without a heavy coat, the air still has a chill to it but the sun hits your back and wraps you in warmth; you feel slightly reborn, as though that fog you've been in for months has just cleared and bikini season is close at hand. Then there's the matching day in the fall: that really brisk afternoon, the one when you consciously feel the wind touch your skin, gentle but firm, as though Mother Nature is giving you a heads-up to enjoy it while you can. The leaves are crispy underfoot, and the air (if you're in the country) smells like wood smoke. That's the day when I think, "bacon and apples." Bacon because of the smoky scent in the air, and apples because, well, it's apple season and I am helpless in front of a selection of fruit with regal names like Pippin, Braeburn, Gravenstein, Northern Spy, Honeycrisp, and McIntosh. Put these two together, add a bit of leftover roast chicken, and suddenly the impending onset of winter becomes palatable—especially if you have a good glass of wine nearby.

1 tablespoon extra virgin olive oil
2 slices good-quality thick-cut bacon, cut into 1/2-inch pieces
1 ball pizza dough (page 16), thawed if frozen
About 3 ounces fresh mozzarella cheese, torn into bite-size pieces
1/2 Granny Smith or other firm, tart apple, very thinly sliced
About 1/2 cup shredded cooked chicken, preferably home-roasted (page 213)
Sea salt and freshly ground pepper

Preheat the oven to 550°F.

In a medium skillet, heat the oil over medium-high heat. Add the bacon, reduce the heat to medium, and cook, stirring occasionally, until the bacon is nicely colored but not too crisp. Use a slotted spoon to transfer the bacon to a small bowl. Reserve the bacon fat.

Shape the pizza crust as directed in the master recipe. Brush the crust evenly with some of the bacon fat, leaving about a 1-inch border all around. Scatter the mozzarella over the pizza, then lay the apple slices over the crust and very lightly brush them with a bit of the remaining bacon fat. Layer the shredded chicken and bacon over the apples and season with salt and pepper.

Transfer the pizza to the oven and bake until the crust is nicely browned, the cheese has melted, and the apples are just beginning to color, 6 to 10 minutes.

WHITE WINE CLAMS WITH PANCETTA AND PARSLEY

If I stumbled on this recipe in a cookbook, my initial instinct would be to turn the page, roll my eyes, and possibly let out a snort of dismay: Why, I would be wondering, did the writer feel the need to take a perfectly wonderful seafood dish and try and force it onto a pizza? I've long been irritated by pizzas that seemed more effortful than necessary, overwrought and overthought concoctions that take classic dishes and try to make them into trendy toppings. But that was until I tasted a clam pizza made with a gentle, barely-there cream sauce, studded with smoky bits of pancetta, and finished with grassy parsley leaves. Suddenly the idea of clams in wine sauce on a crust made perfect sense—the best part is usually dunking the bread in the briny liquid anyway, so why was I so uppity about this? The butter, clam liquor, and wine make a thick, silky sauce that replaces the need for cheese. If you can get over the fact that it feels slightly contrived (like I did), it's absolutely delicious.

1 to 2 tablespoons extra virgin olive oil
¼ pound pancetta, cut into ¼-inch pieces
½ onion, chopped
2 garlic cloves, finely chopped
1 fresh bay leaf
Pinch of red pepper flakes
1 cup dry white wine
2 dozen littleneck or other hard-shell clams, scrubbed
1 tablespoon unsalted butter
1 ball pizza dough (page 16), thawed if frozen
Handful of fresh flat-leaf parsley

Preheat the oven to 550°F.

In a large lidded pot, heat 1 tablespoon of oil over medium-high heat. When the oil is hot, add the pancetta and cook, stirring occasionally, until colored and just crisping on the edges. Use a slotted spoon to transfer the pancetta to a small bowl. Reserve the fat in the pan.

Add the onion to the pancetta fat (if needed, add another 1 tablespoon olive oil), return the pan to medium heat, and sauté until the onion is soft and becomes translucent, about 6 minutes. Add the garlic, bay leaf, and pepper flakes and cook for another 2 to 3 minutes, stirring occasionally. Add the wine, bring to a simmer, add the clams, and cover. Let the clams cook, shaking the pan every few minutes, until all the clams have opened, 10 to 12 minutes (discard any clams that don't open). Transfer the clams to a large bowl to cool and discard the bay leaf. When the clams are cool enough to handle, remove the meat and discard the shells.

While the clams cool, return the pan to medium-high heat and cook the liquid in the pan until there are only 2 to 3 tablespoons left and it is the consistency of syrup, 10 to 15 minutes more. Add the butter and swirl until melted and well combined. Remove from the heat and set aside.

Shape the pizza crust as directed in the master recipe. Brush the crust with the reduced clam sauce, leaving about a 1-inch border all around. Sprinkle the pizza with the pancetta and clams.

Transfer the pizza to the oven and bake until the crust is nicely browned, 6 to 10 minutes. To serve, sprinkle the parsley all over the face of the pie.

Suddenly the idea of clams in wine sauce on a crust made perfect sense—the best part is usually dunking the bread in the briny liquid anyway, so why was I so uppity about this?

CLAMS WITH CREAMY TOMATO SAUCE AND BASIL

Nigel Slater is one of my very favorite food writers. He has a way of making cooking seem like the best reason in the world to get out of bed in the morning, and his food is always appealing to me, even when it's not a combination I would normally be drawn to. His recipes are engaging, and he offers up so many suggestions for varying a dish that you can't help but improvise and feel like you're inventing a meal all your own—with his guidance of course. He is also of the school that believes you can make dinner with what you've got if you have a decent instinct. All of which leads me to how this pizza came to be. It's not borrowed from any of the many recipes of his that I adore. Instead it was born of his influence on how I cook. With a can of clams in the cupboard, a bit of tomato sauce in the freezer, and barely a splash of cream leftover from a day of baking, I heard his voice in my head saying "Seriously, Suzanne, it's just dinner after all." So I took a chance and put it all together. I probably should mention that this happened because I found myself in the rather alarming and quite infrequent situation of being without a box of pasta. Under normal circumstances this combination would have ended up tossed with linguine. But it found its way to a crust. And it was really good. And I owe it all to Mr. Slater for years of encouraging me in the kitchen. The only change I've made since that first experimental effort is to use fresh clams—it's a nice improvement, but not necessary if you're looking for a shortcut.

2 tablespoons extra virgin olive oil

2 garlic cloves, finely chopped

1 cup water

2 dozen littleneck or other hard-shell clams, scrubbed

¼ cup Essential Pomodoro Sauce (page 25)

2 tablespoons heavy cream (or to taste)

Pinch of red pepper flakes (or to taste)

1 ball pizza dough (page 16), thawed if frozen

About 3 ounces fresh mozzarella cheese or burrata, torn into bite-size pieces

Handful of fresh basil leaves, torn

Preheat the oven to 550°F.

In a large lidded pot, heat the oil over medium-high heat. When the oil is hot, add the garlic and cook until just fragrant, 1 to 2 minutes. Add the water and bring to a simmer. Add the clams, cover, and let them cook, shaking the pan every few minutes, until all have opened, 10 to 12 minutes (discard any that don't open). Transfer the clams to a large bowl to cool. When the clams are cool enough to handle, remove the meat and discard the shells.

While the clams cool, in a small saucepan, heat the sauce over medium heat. Add the cream and pepper flakes and cook gently until the flavors begin to meld, 6 to 8 minutes. Remove from the heat.

Shape the pizza crust as directed in the master recipe. Use the back of a spoon to gently smear the creamy tomato sauce over the pizza, leaving about a 1-inch border all around. Scatter the cheese over the sauce, followed by the clams.

Transfer the pizza to the oven and bake until the crust is nicely browned and the cheese has melted, 6 to 10 minutes. To serve, scatter the basil on the pizza.

WALNUT PESTO WITH CHICKEN AND MUSHROOMS

Neither of us can remember where this combination came from, but at some point years ago I started making a pasta with roasted garlic, chicken, mushrooms, and walnuts (see Garlicky Pasta with Chicken, Mushrooms, and Walnuts, page 218). The interesting part of the dish is that half of the walnuts are ground up and added to the roasted garlic while the remainder are toasted and used as a finishing touch, a nice solid crunch in contrast to the other tender textures. I have a love-hate relationship with this pasta. As much as I find it soothing and earthy and wonderful, I also sometimes wish it would just go away. That's because Ken is a creature of habit; it's one of his most endearing and irritating traits. Nearly every time I ask what kind of pasta he wants for dinner, he can be counted on to say something along the lines of: "What about that chicken-walnut-mushroom-garlic one? We haven't had that for a while." Except that usually we have. But I get it. There are those foods that become part of your familial repertoire, the dishes that take on meaning in their own right, the ones you crave when you want to feel coddled; a bowl of linguine as shorthand for home. I totally get that. But sometimes I just need to mix things up. So I took this pasta and turned it into a pizza. Everyone is happy.

2 tablespoons unsalted butter

10 cremini or button mushrooms, trimmed and quartered

Sea salt and freshly ground pepper

1 ball pizza dough (page 16), thawed if frozen

2 to 3 tablespoons Walnut Pesto (page 33)

About 3 ounces fresh mozzarella cheese, torn into bite-size pieces

About 1/2 cup shredded cooked chicken, preferably home-roasted (page 213)

1/4 cup finely grated Parmesan cheese

Leaves from a few sprigs fresh basil, cut into thin ribbons

Preheat the oven to 550°F.

In a large skillet, melt the butter over medium-high heat. Add the mushrooms, season with salt and pepper, and cook, stirring occasionally, until they release their liquid and it evaporates, about 20 minutes total. Continue to cook until the mushrooms are nicely caramelized on all sides. Remove from the heat.

Shape the pizza crust as directed in the master recipe. Use the back of a spoon to smear a couple tablespoons of the pesto evenly over the pizza, leaving a 1-inch border all around. Scatter the cheese over the pesto followed by the mushrooms and chicken. Sprinkle the Parmesan over all.

Transfer the pizza to the oven and bake until the crust is nicely browned and the cheese has melted, 6 to 10 minutes. To serve, sprinkle with the basil.

SARDINES, THYME, AND FENNEL WITH BREADCRUMBS

When I was growing up, our weekend lunches were almost identical to the ones Ken and I have now: a smattering of bits and pieces spread across the counter or table for everyone to pick at. One of my favorite variations on this grazing theme was when my dad would pull a can of sardines out of the pantry, a lemon, and a box of Triscuits. We were the only two who liked sardines and it always felt like a treat, sharing a small can just between us. Claiming it was too sharp for me to do, he'd peel back the tin lid of the can until it curled, exposing the glistening little silvery fish tightly packed in golden oil that we'd then layer on crackers and douse with lemon juice. To this day I still happily eat sardines, bones and all, but as I'm the only sardine fan in the family, it's a less frequent event than I might like. Which is why this pizza is such a treat. The fennel and thyme soften the flavor of the fish for those who don't lust after sardines like I do, and the breadcrumbs add an extra crunch. For me it harkens back to being a kid in Los Angeles, but the flavors are almost pure Mediterranean—think Spain, Greece, and the South of France all bundled together.

3 tablespoons extra virgin olive oil
1 fennel bulb, trimmed and thinly sliced
Sea salt and freshly ground pepper
About ¼ cup of water
1 ball pizza dough (page 16), thawed if frozen
About 3 ounces fresh mozzarella cheese, torn into bite-size pieces
4 to 6 sardines, in olive oil
½ cup fresh breadcrumbs
Leaves from 2 to 3 sprigs fresh thyme

Preheat the oven to 550°F.

In a medium saucepan, heat 2 tablespoons of the olive oil over medium-high heat. When the oil is hot, add the fennel and sprinkle with salt. Reduce the heat to medium and cook, stirring occasionally, until the fennel begins to color, 10 to 15 minutes. When the fennel is just turning brown on the edges, add the water, increase the heat to medium-high, and continue to cook until all the liquid has evaporated and the fennel is very tender and nicely colored, 15 minutes. Remove from the heat.

continued

continued

Shape the pizza crust as directed in the master recipe. Spread the fennel, or as much as you want to use, evenly over the crust, leaving about a 1-inch border all around. Dot the fennel with the mozzarella. Use a fork to gently remove any obvious bones from the sardines and scatter pieces of the fish over the pie.

In a small bowl, toss together the breadcrumbs, the remaining 1 tablespoon olive oil, the thyme, and salt and pepper. Scatter it over the top of the pizza.

Transfer the pizza to the oven and bake until the crust is nicely browned, the cheese has melted, and the breadcrumbs are toasty, 6 to 10 minutes.

Claiming it was too sharp for me to do, he'd peel back the tin lid of the can until it curled, exposing the glistening little silvery fish tightly packed in golden oil.

STICKS *and* OTHER SNACKS

So I have a secret. I steal food. To my mind it's one of the lesser known, or perhaps just more furtive, perks of being the cook in the house. I surreptitiously snack as I cook: an olive here, the crispiest bit of skin off a roast chicken there. It's why I love tapas and mezze so much. I've always enjoyed grazing more than eating a full meal. Perhaps it's a commitment issue. I'm more comfortable nibbling on lots of small bites rather than committing to any one single plate. When it comes to a meal, monogamy is not my thing, with the exception of pizza, I suppose.

Admittedly, this tendency (pathology?) comes out full force when I'm alone in the kitchen. When I find those wonderful marinated artichoke hearts at the Italian delicatessen—the ones with the irresistibly long stems—I can't help but treat myself to a briny bite. And when I'm peeling off tissue paper–thin pieces of prosciutto, can I be blamed for palming a slice and savoring it before everyone else gets theirs? To me, first dibs are a perk of being the cook. Like a shoplifter who can't stop stealing socks, I'm light-fingered when it comes to a slice of avocado intended for a salad or a handful of pine nuts meant for pesto.

Which is why I find the whole notion of snacks before a meal so appealing. Sure I may get caught with a mouthful of Stilton or a smear of sauce on my cheek if you wander into my kitchen unannounced, but put those same bits and pieces on a plate and call them "appetizers," and suddenly it's legitimate: Instead of a sly snacker, I'm simply an attentive host. And when it comes to a prelude for pizza, I find it's often more about the shopping than the cooking. You don't want to ruin dinner with a heavy, overthought, and overwrought snack. You want to give your guests a little something to keep them happy with a glass of wine. A plate of good salami and a dish of olives will do the trick, a couple of fresh figs alongside a sliver of Manchego counts, and a handful of spiced nuts or a simple crostini is often more than enough.

I tend to make my snacks in advance, sometimes a day or more. A small jar of pâté or marinated beans can be done ahead of time, as can some homemade crackers. A can of chickpeas can be popped open and fried up while you wait for people to arrive. Many of the recipes in this section rely on the very same ingredients in the pizzas—so you don't have to think about an entirely separate grocery list when it comes to company. If you're keeping your pantry stocked for pizza, you'll probably have something floating around to help pull a predinner nibble together, too.

To my mind, the socially acceptable snacking known as "appetizers" is one of the most enjoyable parts of cooking and eating. It's almost as much fun as covertly poaching that idle fig when no one is looking.

TARALLI

Makes about 40

I have a very soft spot for foreign grocery stores. One of the first things Ken and I do when we travel to a new place is to find a market to buy some staples. Instead of dashing in and continuing on our way, we both inevitably end up wandering the aisles in awe of all the wonderfully unfamiliar fare. The packaging always seems more interesting, the food itself is enchanting, and suddenly what was supposed to be a quick stop for bottled water becomes a full-fledged sightseeing tour. This is actually one reason we love to rent apartments or cottages when we travel, so we can indulge and actually buy stuff at these exotic emporiums full of edible adventure. Which is exactly what happened when we were in Umbria. While foraging for provisions at the local market, we stumbled on these little breadstick-like, cracker-esque, pretzel-y snacks called taralli. They're addictive and that perfect little nibble you need when you don't want to spoil dinner but do want something to go with your wine. When we got back to New York, we started noticing them in our local gourmet shops, but that didn't keep me from wanting to make my own. After doing some research, I found that some recipes use yeast and some don't, some have a bit of chew and some are more crunchy. Most relied on a two-stage cooking process of boiling and then baking. Ken and I played around using my pizza dough as a base recipe until we got what we wanted: a crunchy, slightly salty snack that only needs 20 minutes of resting time.

½ cup dry white wine
½ cup water
390 grams bread flour (about 2¾ cups)
2 teaspoons sea salt
¼ cup extra virgin olive oil

In a small saucepan, combine the wine and water and set over low heat until it feels warm to the touch.

Put the flour and salt in a food processor and turn the machine on. Add the oil through the feed tube first, then add the warmed wine mixture in a slow, steady stream. Continue to process for 2 to 3 minutes (the dough should form a ball and ride around in the processor).

Lay a piece of plastic wrap about 12 inches long on a clean work surface. Use your hands to press the dough on the plastic wrap into an 8 x 6-inch rectangle. Cover the dough with plastic wrap and let it rest (you want the gluten to relax) for 20 minutes.

Bring a large pot of water to a boil. Line 2 baking sheets with parchment paper.

continued

continued

While the water comes to a boil, cut the dough in half lengthwise and then continue to cut each of those long pieces in half again until you have 8 long ropes. Cut the ropes crosswise into 2-inch pieces. Stretch each piece gently and form it into a ring, pressing the two ends together to seal. Place the rings on the prepared baking sheets.

Preheat the oven to 400°F.

Working in batches, gently add the taralli to the boiling water. When they float, allow them to boil for another minute. Use a slotted spoon to transfer them to a wire rack so the water doesn't pool on the baking sheets. When all of the taralli have been boiled, transfer them back to the parchment-lined baking sheets.

Bake the taralli until golden, 20 to 30 minutes. Remove from the oven, let cool, and snack. These are best the day they're made.

I have a very soft spot for foreign grocery stores. One of the first things Ken and I do when we travel to a new place is to find a market to buy some staples. Instead of dashing in and continuing on our way, we both inevitably end up wandering the aisles in awe of all the wonderfully unfamiliar fare.

KNOBBY BREADSTICKS

Makes 24

A friend of mine in college first made these for me, and I was immediately smitten by them. He was an incredibly soft-spoken guy, yet an almost tangible aura of adventure seemed to hover around him—like he'd seen much of the world already, and our small Central Coast town was just a brief layover en route to his next exotic locale. His bookshelves were lined with Milan Kundera novels, collections of poetry by Donne and Carver, and impenetrable volumes by Heidegger; he skipped beer in favor of claret-colored wine; and maybe most magical of all, he crafted small, handmade books of his inky line drawings, bound up with bits of delicate twine. And he served these breadsticks one night (along with the first tagine I had ever tasted). They were rustic in shape, like long arthritic fingers, but elegant at the same time. He served them standing up in a tall Mason jar in the middle of the table, like a bouquet of edible flowers, the way I still serve them to this day. If you like a thicker breadstick, you can certainly cut fewer and just stretch them longer and leave them even knobbier—just know that you'll have to increase the cooking time by a few minutes. You can also add flavor to them if you want to play around. I've mixed in grated Parmesan, fennel seeds, and even crumbled a bit of flake salt or freshly ground pepper on them just before baking, all with good results.

½ cup whole milk
½ cup water
390 grams bread flour (about 2¾ cups)
1½ teaspoons active dry yeast
2 teaspoons sea salt
¼ cup extra virgin olive oil

In a small saucepan, combine the milk and water and set over low heat until it feels warm to the touch.

Put the flour, yeast, and salt in a food processor and turn the machine on. Add the oil through the feed tube first, then add the warmed milk mixture in a slow, steady stream. Continue to process for 2 to 3 minutes (the dough should form a ball and ride around in the processor).

Lay a piece of plastic wrap about 12 inches long on a clean work surface. Use your hands to press the dough on the plastic wrap into an 8 x 6-inch rectangle. Press your fingers into the top of the dough all over it, making indentations as though it were a focaccia. With the long side facing you, fold the left third of the dough over and repeat the finger indentions on this folded section. Fold the right third over (as you would a letter) and use your fingers to make the indentations again. Cover the folded dough with plastic wrap and let rise for 20 minutes.

Line 2 baking sheets with parchment paper. Cut the dough in half so you have two squares of dough. Cut each of the squares in half again and continue in this manner until you have 24 thin ropes of dough. Gently roll and stretch each piece of dough into an 8- to 10-inch rope. Lay the ropes on the baking sheets. Don't fret if the ropes are uneven—you want them to be knobby and organic in shape. Cover the baking sheets lightly with plastic wrap and let the breadsticks rest for 30 minutes, or until they are slightly puffed.

Preheat the oven to 400°F.

Remove the plastic wrap from the baking sheets and transfer them to the oven. Bake for 10 to 15 minutes, then roll or flip the breadsticks so they have a chance to color on all sides. Continue baking until they're nicely golden brown, another 10 to 15 minutes. Remove from the oven, transfer to a rack, and let cool. These are undoubtedly best the day they're made but will hold for a day or so in an airtight container.

They were rustic in shape, like long arthritic fingers, but elegant at the same time. He served them standing up in a tall Mason jar in the middle of the table, like a bouquet of edible flowers.

MARINATED GIGANTE BEANS

Serves 6 to 8

These beans are one of my favorite parlor tricks. They're ridiculously easy and always leave people asking for the recipe. I hate to admit this, but while they're of course best with dried beans you cook yourself, I almost never bother to do this. I should be ashamed, I know, but we tend to entertain kind of spontaneously and suddenly I need a snack to serve in a few hours and don't want to run to the store. So I grab a can of these big creamy beans from the cupboard, chop up a few jarred pepperoncinis I keep in the fridge, smash a clove or two of garlic, and run out to the oregano pot to clip some fresh herbs. With about 10 minutes of prep time and no cooking, I have a jar of beans and need nothing more than a smattering of toothpicks to go with them.

1 can (14 ounces) gigante beans, drained and rinsed, or ½ cup dried beans cooked until tender
½ cup extra virgin olive oil
Grated zest and juice of 1 lemon
2 or 3 garlic cloves, peeled and smashed
4 to 6 pepperoncini, trimmed and finely chopped
1 to 2 sprigs fresh oregano leaves, roughly chopped
2 to 3 tablespoons sherry or other bright vinegar
Sea salt and freshly ground pepper

Put the beans in a canning jar large enough to hold the other ingredients as well. Add the oil, lemon zest, lemon juice, garlic, pepperoncini, and oregano. Stir gently to combine so you don't smash the beans and taste for brightness. Add enough vinegar to give the marinade a bit of tang but not to overpower—they will get stronger as they sit.

Season the beans with salt and pepper and seal the jar. Let sit in the fridge for an hour or two, or overnight if possible. Give the jar a gentle shake every now and then to circulate the vinaigrette. Taste again and adjust the seasoning as needed.

Serve with toothpicks for spearing (watch out for the smashed cloves of garlic, as they look remarkably like the beans after some time in the jar).

PROSCIUTTO WITH ASPARAGUS AND ARUGULA ROLLS

(aka the Superhero Snack)

Serves 4

Our friend Al helped us build our pizza oven a couple of years ago. He also turned a hideous olive green bathroom circa 1972 into my favorite room in our small house. After we tore the heinous beige rug out of our bedroom this year, he laid beautiful wide-plank wood floors for us. I once called him on a bitter cold December afternoon, desperate, because water was spraying out of the back of the fridge; he arrived in under an hour to fix it. He's saved us from floods caused by melting snow when we weren't around, and he's gifted us with more than a few wine-soaked evenings listening to country music on the patio and eating these little snacks. When he shows up carrying a big orange Home Depot bucket, we never know if it will be full of tools or icy bottles of Albariño. Happily, often it's both. Sure some people have fairy godmothers, but we have a superhero named Al, and he has his own official appetizer—barely blanched or roasted asparagus tangled up with baby greens, lightly dressed in lemon and olive oil, and all rolled up like Italian sushi. The only key to this recipe is making sure you get prosciutto that's cut well; if it's tattered and torn, you won't be able to get the chiffon-thin sheets to layer well.

Salt and freshly ground pepper
1 pound pencil-thin asparagus, trimmed
3 tablespoons extra virgin olive oil
½ teaspoon grated lemon zest
1 tablespoon fresh lemon juice
A couple handfuls baby or wild arugula
16 thin slices prosciutto (about ½ pound),
    each about 8 inches long

Bring a large pot of salted water to a boil. Add the asparagus to the pot and cook until bright green and just tender, about 3 minutes depending on thickness. Drain the asparagus and run it immediately under cold water to stop the cooking process.

In a large bowl, whisk together the oil, lemon zest, lemon juice, and salt and pepper. Add the arugula and asparagus spears to the bowl and toss gently to coat, being careful not to snap the asparagus.

On a large cutting board or work surface, arrange 4 slices of the prosciutto vertically and slightly overlapping to form a rectangle, about 6 by 8 inches. Lay one-quarter of the dressed arugula and asparagus horizontally across the prosciutto on the end closest to you. Tightly roll up the prosciutto as you would a jelly-roll, being sure to keep the vegetables evenly distributed.

Cut the rolls on the bias into 8 pieces. Repeat with the remaining ingredients.

KEN'S CRÈME BRÛLÉED ALMONDS

Serves 8 to 12

I came home from a photo shoot once with a very expensive tin of almonds. They were supposedly crème brûlée–flavored, and Ken fell hard for them. We found them online, but they were prohibitively expensive (think foie gras or caviar, just in nut form). So we looked at the ingredients list and started playing around. The truth is, what we came up with doesn't really look like those fancy ones, which were delicately dusted with a fine sugar coating. These are heartier, more like a brittle, but the same seductive crème brûlée flavor is here—and while I think they could work crumbled over ice cream, Ken is a devoted fan of them set in a dish, next to a glass of full-bodied red wine, in front of a televised soccer game (preferably one featuring Manchester United).

¼ cup sweetened condensed milk
2 tablespoons unsalted butter
2 tablespoons sugar
1 tablespoon vanilla extract
1 teaspoon sea salt, plus more for dusting
1 vanilla bean
2 cups unsalted roasted almonds

Preheat the oven to 300°F. Line a baking sheet with parchment paper.

In a medium saucepan, combine the condensed milk, butter, sugar, vanilla, and salt and bring to a simmer over medium heat.

Meanwhile, use a sharp paring knife to slice the vanilla bean lengthwise just deep enough to peel open the pod like a book. Use the knife to scrape out the sticky vanilla seeds inside the pod—this is easiest if you run your knife down the interior, flattening out the vanilla pod as you go, like you were buttering bread. Add the vanilla seeds to the milk mixture and stir to combine thoroughly. The seeds tend to stick together in little clumps, so whisk well until the little brown flecks are evenly distributed. (I save my scraped pod and add it to our sugar bowl so we have vanilla-infused sugar for coffee).

When the mixture is just beginning to simmer, remove it from the heat and add the almonds. Toss the almonds until they are well coated, then transfer them to the prepared baking sheet. Use a spatula to spread the coated almonds into an even layer and sprinkle with a bit more salt (I use flake salt here) if desired. Bake until the coating begins to bubble and turn slightly brown, 20 to 25 minutes. Use a spatula to toss them around and cook for another 10 to 15 minutes until they are rich in color.

Remove from the oven and let the almonds cool completely on the pan— they will crisp up as the sugar cools. Taste and sprinkle with salt if needed, and serve or keep in an airtight container for up to a month.

Ken is a devoted fan of them set in a dish, next to a glass of full-bodied red wine, in front of a televised soccer game (preferably one featuring Manchester United).

CHICKEN LIVER PÂTÉ

Serves 6 to 8

Every now and then, as a treat for my dad, my mom used to make chopped chicken liver. Against all normal kid-like behavior, I loved it. As I got older, I became partial to most pâtés and terrines, but my favorite has always remained those derived from chicken livers. I still like the deli-style chopped liver, but what I make—and what I prefer—is this über-smooth and creamy chicken liver pâté. I admit this gets slightly fussy—you have to commit to the tedious task of pressing it through a fine sieve—but it really does make the difference between a good but grainy pâté and a sublimely smooth one. This is probably why I only make this a couple of times a year, but it's one of those recipes that make me feel like I am really cooking, like I'm making something a sophisticated Frenchwoman might whip up on a whim between the cassoulet and the soufflé. It's not that it's hard, it's just technique-oriented, which I kind of love. It's perfect served with toasted baguette slices, any decent crackers, and, if truth be told, spooned right out of the jar when no one else is watching (the day after you've served it to company, of course).

8 tablespoons (1 stick) unsalted butter, at room temperature
1 onion, chopped
1 pound chicken livers
Sea salt
⅓ cup heavy cream
1 tablespoon fresh thyme leaves
2 to 3 tablespoons brandy (to taste)
Freshly ground pepper

In a medium skillet, melt 2 tablespoons of the butter over medium-high heat. Add the onion and cook until softened but not coloring, about 4 minutes. Add the livers, sprinkle with salt, and cook until they begin to brown, about 3 minutes. Flip them and cook until the second side browns but the inside is still relatively pink. If you're not sure about how the livers are cooking, cut into one and check.

Transfer the livers and onion to a food processor, including all the buttery juices from the pan (reserve the pan). Add 4 tablespoons of the softened butter, the cream, and thyme and puree until smooth. Add the brandy to the pan you fried the livers in and set it over high heat to deglaze and cook off some of the alcohol. Add the brandy to the liver mixture and pulse a few times to combine. Add some pepper, taste, and adjust the seasoning if needed.

continued

continued

Set a fine-mesh sieve over a large bowl. Pour the liver puree into the sieve (you may have to work in batches depending on the size of your sieve) and use a rubber spatula to press the mixture through the sieve. Once the mixture is velvety smooth, transfer it to a canning jar. Smooth the top and set aside.

In a small saucepan, melt the remaining 2 tablespoons butter and spoon off any foam. Pour the melted butter over the top of the pâté (this will harden, turn into a seal, and will keep the livers from discoloring). Cover and transfer the jar to the fridge to set up, ideally overnight. Once the butter seal is broken, you can keep the pâté covered in the jar for a of couple days.

This is one of those recipes that make me feel like I am really cooking, like I'm making something a sophisticated Frenchwoman might whip up on a whim between the cassoulet and the soufflé.

TUNA TARTARE ON SALTY POTATO CHIPS

Serves 6 to 8

All cooks have their repertoire of recipes that they pull out time and again. Some because they're family favorites; some because they're really fast, easy, and reliable; and some because they dazzle guests. This one fits into all the above categories. It's one of my go-to, impress-the-guests snacks because while it's very simple, it's got a bit of restaurant flair without the fuss. This is adapted from a much fancier, more chef-y recipe by Eric Ripert of Le Bernardin fame, so if you really want to do it right, you should just get his book and use his recipe—it's that good. But if you're someone who's more comfy in jeans and flip-flops (like me) than a pencil skirt and high heels, this version will make you happy. I forgo Ripert's ginger-infused oil, wasabi powder, and artful pressing of the tuna into a circular mold to be drizzled with oil, dappled with tomatoes, and topped with a single chip (all of which is stunningly delicious and beautiful). Instead, I prefer to toss the tuna with a few other fresh ingredients and call it a day. I suppose if one were in a cheeky mood, this dumbed-down version could be considered "chips and dip." It still seems to maintain its power to impress.

1 pound sushi-grade tuna, trimmed of any tough bits and cut into $1/8$-inch dice
3 tablespoons neutral oil, such as grapeseed
Grated zest of 1 lemon
1 tablespoon fresh lemon juice (or more to taste)
2 tablespoons finely chopped fresh cilantro
$1/2$ jalapeño chile, seeded if desired and finely diced
1 teaspoon toasted sesame seeds
2 scallions (white parts only), finely diced
Sea salt and freshly ground pepper
Good-quality salted potato chips (I like the kettle-cooked ones)

Not more than an hour or so before you plan to serve this, put the tuna in a bowl and toss gently with the oil, lemon zest, lemon juice, cilantro, jalapeño, sesame seeds, and scallions. Season with salt and pepper and taste. Adjust the seasoning as necessary—depending on how flavorful your tuna is, you may need more lemon juice or salt and pepper.

Scoop a generous tablespoon of the tartare onto the potato chips and serve immediately.

TANGLED PARSNIP RIBBONS

For one of my so-called "big" birthdays, we were living up in Connecticut and one of my oldest and closest friends, Jackie, flew in from London to celebrate. Needless to say, it was a 4-day weekend of too much—too much food, too much wine, too much lost sleep, too much coffee to make up for the lost sleep . . . you get the picture. But it was fabulous, and among the many meals we cooked together was my actual birthday dinner: an herb and breadcrumb–crusted rack of lamb, sage roasted-and-smashed potatoes, braised leeks, and, as a starter, these addictive parsnip ribbons. Jackie had stumbled on the recipe in a magazine and decided they were the perfect snack to accompany the beautiful champagne she had procured. They were, and still are, one of my very favorites, though I've taken some liberties with the recipe along the way. Unbelievably simple yet unexpected, they're also really beautiful on the plate, a slightly charred bramble of creamy ribbons all knotted up in an almost sculptural way.

4 medium parsnips, trimmed and peeled
2 tablespoons extra virgin olive oil
½ cup grated Parmesan cheese
1 to 2 tablespoons fresh thyme leaves
Sea salt and freshly ground pepper

Preheat the oven to 400°F.

Use a vegetable peeler to slice the parsnips lengthwise into long ribbons. This is easiest if you rotate the parsnip every few pulls, peeling on all sides evenly. Eventually you'll hit the core, which you can discard.

Transfer the parsnip ribbons to a baking sheet and toss them with the oil, Parmesan, thyme, and salt and pepper. Bake the ribbons until they begin to brown, 12 to 15 minutes. Toss and continue to bake until nice and crispy and tangled, another 12 to 15 minutes.

Serve immediately with an additional sprinkle of cheese or thyme if desired.

SWEET PEA CROSTINI WITH PECORINO

Serves 8

I find certain parts of cooking very much like yoga. I can get lost in the process, especially if it's repetitive, and wander (mentally) off to a less chaotic, more mindful place. Kneading bread does it for me, stirring risotto can work, but one of the best ways to zone out (mindfully) in the kitchen is with peas. Yes, there is a Zen calm to be captured in the repetitive shelling of peas. And while I am constantly striving for calmness in life, it's secondary to my other constant goal of consuming something delicious. So when I stumble across peas at the farmers' market, my yogic side is subsumed by my hunger and I'm a bit like a shopaholic at the Barneys Warehouse sale, elbowing (mindfully) to the front of the crowd to claim my fair share. Some women lust after the season's hottest kitten heel; I'm a sucker for rhubarb, ramps, and, yes, English peas. Sadly, like so many of my favorite things, there are only a few fleeting weeks when peas are really sweet, so more often than not I have to be okay with skipping the meditative aspect of this dish and grabbing a box of frozen peas (captured at their peak, frozen are often sweeter than their fresh cousins, believe it or not). Either way, this crostini is a terrific bite before pizza—in the spring after a restorative shelling practice or in the depths of winter when a trip to the freezer section has to do. (And, yes, this recipe is based on the same risi e bisi recipe I've adapted to the pizza on page 92. What can I say? When peas are mashed up with butter and Parmesan, they're really good.)

4 tablespoons unsalted butter, at room temperature
2 cups fresh or frozen peas
¼ cup good-quality chicken stock (preferably homemade)
Sea salt and freshly ground pepper
8 thick slices rustic bread
2 to 3 ounces pecorino cheese, shaved
Fresh mint leaves

Preheat the broiler.

In a medium saucepan, melt 1 tablespoon of the butter over medium-high heat. Add the peas and swirl to coat them in the butter, then add the chicken stock. Bring the stock to a simmer and cook just until the peas turn bright green, 1 or 2 minutes. Remove the pan from the heat.

With a slotted spoon, transfer half the peas to a bowl and set aside. Put the remaining peas and their cooking liquid in a food processor or blender and puree. Add the remaining 3 tablespoons butter and continue to process until smooth. Season with salt and pepper.

Lay the sliced bread on a baking sheet and toast under the broiler until just beginning to brown on the edges.

Spread a dollop of the pea puree over the toasts and smear to the edges. Top each crostini with a generous sprinkling of the reserved whole peas, a few shavings of pecorino, and fresh mint leaves to serve.

FRIED CHICKPEAS WITH PIMENTÓN

Serves 6 to 8

We were lost in that surreal, heady place where jet lag takes you—the disorienting space that exists courtesy of lost sleep, muddled hours, and too much caffeine. But we were also in Spain, and though it was colder than we'd hoped, oranges hung from the trees and the high-pitched chirp of small birds followed us everywhere. Some sang out from ornate wire cages on terraces while others roamed freely, chasing one another among the minarets. We wandered the curvy streets of Seville after dropping our bags, because even though exhausted, who can rationalize sleep in a new city when the day is still bright? But after a couple of hours, as even the most resilient traveler knows, the journey takes its toll and you have no choice but to give in. We woke up at 10 p.m., almost exactly the time we would have been going to sleep at home, so all bets were off. Getting on schedule was a lost cause. Or was it? Ken reminded me that we were in Spain—they don't even leave the house till this hour, the guidebooks promised. Contrary to every fiber of our conventional selves, we dressed and left our bed in search of something, well, Spanish. What we found was a startlingly chilly wind, one that pushed us down dark, winding cobblestone streets lined with tiled walls. Then, around a corner, maybe two, a tapas bar glowed from within, cloudy with cigarette smoke—the very idea of which at home would repel but instead curled around us and lured us inside. Persuaded that

a glass of sherry was the only appropriate drink at a time and in a place like this, we stood pressed up against the bar eating as though it had been days, not hours, since our last meal. A half ración of Ibérico ham, meaty green olives, garlicky shrimp in oil so hot it continued to bubble in the dish, and a bowl of fried chickpeas. These are those chickpeas—or as best as I can replicate them.

1 can (15.5 ounces) chickpeas, drained and rinsed
3 tablespoons extra virgin olive oil
Sea salt and freshly ground pepper
1 tablespoon smoked paprika

Gently pat the chickpeas dry between paper towels (if the chickpeas are wet, they won't crisp up).

In a skillet large enough to hold the chickpeas in an even layer, heat the oil over high heat. When the oil is hot, add the chickpeas, sprinkle with some salt and pepper, and reduce the heat to medium. Continue to cook the chickpeas until nicely roasted and firm, shaking the pan every few minutes to make sure they brown on all sides, 20 to 25 minutes. Sprinkle with the paprika and toss to coat evenly.

Transfer to a shallow dish and serve with toothpicks for spearing.

FRICO WITH FRESH FIGS

For my birthday one year Ken bought me a small fig tree. Not being terribly original, we took to calling it "Figgy" (we had recently planted a lime seed from one of the limes in my parents' garden and were calling that fledgling botanical "Limey," so it seemed appropriate). Figgy arrived home from the nursery with three figs dangling from her boney branches. I was ecstatic to watch these little orbs ripen and taste my first homegrown fig, but within a day of sitting on the deck the local gang of squirrels had raided our entire crop. Alas. In the winter we brought Figgy inside to survive the cold and she dropped all her leaves almost immediately. For most of the next 6 months she looked like one of those hangman illustrations, sticks poking out in all directions, naked of any green. Then in March she leafed out beautifully and I waited with bated breath for my figs to appear. They didn't. Another year went by and the process repeated itself; lost leaves, abundant green foliage, no figs. The following year I tried something I read in a gardening book about not watering her all winter so she'd go dormant and produce fruit in the spring. This didn't work either and things took a turn for the worse: I killed her. A year later we bought a second fig tree (affectionately referred to as Figgy Deux) and I killed her, too. So I've resorted to dreaming of the day when I live in a place where mature fig trees are abundant and self-sufficient so I can enjoy their bounty without hurting them. I've also come to acknowledge that when I want them, I have to seek out those perfectly ripe, syrupy figs with bruised-colored flesh. Then I buy as many as I can rationalize, knowing I'll gently cart them home and make fricos to eat with them. Delicate wafers woven out of piquant Parmesan, fricos are nothing more than mounds of cheese baked until melted and then allowed to crisp up. If you don't covet figs like I do, they're a perfect accompaniment to ripe cherry tomatoes or sliced stone fruit, too.

1 generous cup freshly grated Parmesan cheese
4 fresh figs, quartered

Preheat the oven to 375°F. Line a baking sheet with parchment paper.

Scoop tablespoon mounds of Parmesan onto the mat and gently spread the mounds into rough 3-inch rounds being sure to leave at least 1 inch between the rounds. Bake until the cheese has melted and is lightly browned, about 5 minutes. Working quickly, remove the baking sheet from the oven and lift the fricos from the mat with a thin spatula, draping them over a rolling pin. As they cook, the fricos will set up and hold their shape. You can also roll them around the handle of a wooden spoon and shape like a tuile.

To serve, place a quarter of a fig in each frico arch or alongside the crisp.

KOREAN-STYLE CUCUMBER CRAB ROLLS

A remarkable woman and her mother taught me how to make these rolls. I met her at the Union Square Greenmarket (she was the only vendor who regularly had shishito peppers, which I adore when they're fried till blistering, dappled in char, and sprinkled with salt), and we struck up a weekly conversation. Coincidentally, another friend whom I had met while working in the kitchen at a local restaurant had also become friends with her, and one summer day the two of us took a day trip to her farm for lunch. Her farm was everything I imagined an idyllic working farm would be: rambling white farmhouse off in the distance (with requisite wraparound porch), muddy but manicured fields of ripening tomatoes and bushy basil, our farmer friend in her wide-brimmed straw hat walking the rows of melon and squash and talking about companion crops and growing seasons—it was pretty perfect. And then came lunch and it got better. Our farmer's mother served us zucchini pancakes nearly effervescent they were so delicate, wedges of white honeydew, ghostly pale and preternaturally sweet, as well as these incredible crab rolls, paper-thin slivers of chilled cucumber wrapped around sesame-dressed and chili-spiced crab. Served like sushi rolls, the only tricks to this recipe are to wring as much liquid from the cucumbers as you can without tearing them and then freeze the rolls for a bit so they're easier to slice.

2 English cucumbers (a little more than you need, but some of the slices will tear)
2 teaspoons sea salt
6 ounces lump crabmeat
1 Thai chile, seeded if desired and finely diced
1 scallion, finely diced
2 tablespoons sesame oil
Salt and freshly ground pepper

Slice the cucumbers crosswise as thinly as possible while still keeping the rounds whole. Put the slices in a colander set over a bowl, sprinkle with the salt, and let sit for 30 minutes.

Squeeze as much water as you can from the cucumbers over the sieve. Then press them again between paper towels to remove as much moisture as possible, but be careful not to tear the tender slices.

In a bowl, combine the crab, chile, scallion, and oil and season with salt and pepper.

continued

continued

Lay a piece of plastic wrap about 12 inches long on a work surface. Layer the squeezed cucumber slices in a slightly overlapping row across the plastic wrap. Then, make a second row of slices, partially overlapping the first, like fish scales. Continue layering the cucumber this way until you have a square about 6 inches by 6 inches.

Lay the crab mixture horizontally along the bottom of the square and, using the plastic wrap to hold it in place, roll the cucumber around itself, like a sushi roll, keeping it as tight as possible. Twist the ends of the plastic wrap to secure it and put the tube in the freezer.

When the roll is firm enough to slice, cut straight through the plastic wrap (which is kept on to preserve the shape) into 1-inch pieces. Remove the plastic wrap from each piece and serve.

(Full disclosure: The farmer's mother shared this recipe with us in Korean and her daughter translated. I took mental notes between mouthfuls, so any errors are all mine.)

BRUSCHETTA WITH GREEN OLIVE TAPENADE AND BRESAOLA

Serves 8

I always thought that tapenade was about olives. But then I learned that tapenade comes from the French word for capers, tapenas, and my whole notion of the condiment changed. And then it changed back. I like capers, but I like olives more—and while I hate those new-fangled olive bars so prominent in grocery store deli sections, I do get giddy standing in front of the range of different olives, slick with olive oil or brine at my favorite specialty store (Murray's Cheese on Bleecker, for anyone remotely curious). So, after fiddling around with many recipes, increasing the amount of capers and mashing up all colors and flavors of olives, I still believe the dominant flavor in a good tapenade should be the soft, buttery, slightly briny tang of good olives. But one thing has changed: my mashing technique. For a long time I held firm that tapenade should be made as our culinary foremothers and fathers had made it, by smashing it to bits with a mortar and pestle. But why? I had been making homemade mayonnaise with a food processor for ages, blitzing up pesto and salsa the easy way for eons, so why was I so insistent on the old-school approach when it came to tapenade? The world shifted; I wised up, whispered a few words of apology to my beautiful olive wood mortar and pestle, and whipped up a delicious tapenade in mere minutes. Draped with a slice of earthy bresaola and smeared on lightly charred toast, this is a boldly flavored and (almost) traditionally prepared pre-pizza snack.

1 cup Cerignola, Picholine, or other green olives, pitted
1 tablespoon capers, drained and rinsed
1 garlic clove
1 oil-packed anchovy fillet
Leaves from 1 sprig fresh thyme
Leaves from 1 sprig fresh oregano
Grated zest of 1 lemon
¼ cup extra virgin olive oil, plus more for brushing
Fresh lemon juice
Freshly ground pepper
8 thick slices rustic bread
8 thin slices bresaola

Preheat a grill or the broiler.

In a food processor, combine the olives, capers, garlic, anchovy, thyme, oregano, and lemon zest and pulse until coarsely chopped. With the machine running, add the olive oil through the feed tube until the mixture is well combined and nearly smooth. Taste and add lemon juice and pepper as needed. Transfer the tapenade to a lidded jar and use immediately or refrigerate for up to a week.

Brush the bread with a bit of olive oil. Either grill the bread lightly or toast it in the broiler until just golden on the edges.

Smear the toast generously with the tapenade and drape the toasts with a slice of bresaola to serve.

GRILLED PEACHES WITH PROSCIUTTO AND MINT

Serves 8

Everyone has her own idea of the perfect summer day. My memories of summer are varied. Growing up in Los Angeles, summer comes back to me as sitting under a yellow vinyl umbrella and watching the Pacific shimmer. Dry heat blistered the hills, causing them to blur in the haze, while my mom handed out cold peaches, the juice leaving my hands sticky, and the pits of which I'd bury in the burning sand. A few years later, summer meant sipping Diet Coke at lifeguard station number eight with my best friend, Andi, basting ourselves with Hawaiian Tropic dark tanning oil, and wistfully watching the handsome volleyball players dive at the net. But then I moved East. Now summer is sultry and humid, we sit on the patio, and wineglasses dangle from our hands as we linger over a crisp white, or maybe it's rose. We talk until the dragonflies come out. We eat what we can cook outside in the pizza oven or on the grill, anything to keep the house cool. Prosciutto-wrapped melon would be a traditional start to a midsummer pizza dinner, so this recipe really isn't much of a stretch. But like the peaches of my California childhood, these must be truly ripe, weepingly juicy, and radiantly sweet. The roasting process brings out the sugar and adds a delightful caramelized edge to the fruit. However, if the peaches are at that perfect point and you're completely drained by the heat, you can serve them raw if you want, touched only by the tender ham, that final burst of mint like a much-needed dip in the sea.

4 ripe peaches, quartered
2 tablespoons extra virgin olive oil
8 slices prosciutto, torn in half
Leaves from a few sprigs fresh mint, torn

Preheat a grill.

Lay the peaches cut-side up on a baking sheet and brush them with the oil. When the grill is hot, transfer the fruit, cut-side up, to the grill and cook until the fruit begins to soften, about 5 minutes. Flip the peaches and cook the exposed flesh until char-marked. Remove from the heat and let sit until cool enough to handle.

Wrap each piece of peach in a strip of prosciutto and set on a serving plate. Scatter the mint over the peaches.

PARMESAN SHORTBREAD

Makes about 24 2-inch crackers

The first trip abroad that Ken and I took together was to Ireland. We started in Dublin and meandered across the country to Galway and eventually down to Dingle in hopes of hiking—in March. It wasn't the best-laid plan to begin with and the weather didn't cooperate; Dingle in March, as anyone who takes the time to read the guidebook would know, is cold, foggy, and drippy. So instead of trekking the battered cliffs, we ended up taking long lunches, eating potato and leek soup with slabs of brown bread, sipping pints of Guinness in cozy pubs, and reading books in the slightly tattered and faded manor house where we were staying. For dinner we'd stay in our room enjoying the misty views. The owner of the inn kept peacocks, and we sat captivated as they wandered around, their gem-colored tails fanning out like fireworks every now and again. Still full from our late lunch in town, we'd make gin and tonics in small water glasses, stirring our drinks with long, thin Irish pretzels we'd found in the local market, a new take on the swizzle stick. I mention the pretzels because we are both very fond of good salty snacks—not salty junk food, mind you, but good-quality breadsticks, crackers, or pretzels. Something crunchy to accompany a drink or get you through that pang of hunger between lunch and dinner. These cheesy crackers are not remotely like those makeshift swizzle sticks, but they're certainly suitable accompaniments for a good gin and tonic.

1 cup all-purpose flour, plus more for rolling
½ teaspoon sea salt, plus more for sprinkling
½ cup finely grated Parmesan cheese
4 tablespoons unsalted butter, cut into small pieces
¼ cup heavy cream or half-and-half, plus more as needed

Preheat the oven to 400°F. Line a baking sheet with parchment paper.

In a food processor, combine the flour, salt, Parmesan, and butter and pulse until the dry ingredients and the butter are combined and look like coarse meal. Add the cream and let the machine run until the mixture comes together but isn't sticky. You may have to add more liquid a tablespoon at a time until you reach the desired consistency.

On a lightly floured surface, roll the dough into a ¼-inch-thick rectangle that will fit on your baking sheet. If the dough sticks, add a bit more flour. Drape the dough over the rolling pin and gently transfer it to the prepared baking sheet. Use a pizza cutter to lightly score the dough into squares or rectangles and sprinkle with a bit more sea salt if desired.

Bake the crackers until lightly browned, about 10 minutes. Cool on a rack before serving (they will crisp up as they sit).

ROSEMARY AND FLAKE SALT FLATBREADS

I'm always amazed and thrilled by homemade crackers. It's goofy, I realize, but they're always so easy and so much better than anything in a package. These rustic flatbreads are no exception. I started making these when I was working with Mark Bittman. We tested and tested to get this very delicate and very rich combination just right. He likened them to olive oil matzoh, but I've added fresh rosemary and flake salt, so to me, this version resembles something more Italian. They're also really delicious with a generous sprinkle of za'atar (a Middle Eastern seasoning of thyme, sesame seeds, and sumac), if you're in the mood for a hit of the exotic.

⅓ cup extra virgin olive oil
½ cup water
2 cups all-purpose flour, plus more for rolling
½ teaspoon sea salt
2 tablespoons fresh rosemary leaves
Flake sea salt (optional)

Preheat the oven to 500°F.

In a measuring cup, combine the oil and water. Put the flour and salt in a food processor and turn the machine on. Add the olive oil mixture through the feed tube and continue to process until the dough forms a firm ball, rides around on the blade, and is not at all sticky.

Cut the dough into 12 small balls and flatten each into a 3- to 4-inch patty. On a well-floured surface, with a rolling pin, roll each piece of dough into a 6- to 8-inch round. The shapes can and should be irregular, but the dough should be so thin you can practically see through it. Top each piece with some of the rosemary and roll the leaves into the dough as best you can.

Baking in batches, transfer the flatbreads to baking sheets, sprinkle with a bit of flake sea salt if you like, and bake until just puffing up and beginning to brown, 2 to 3 minutes. Flip the breads and cook for another minute or so. Be careful though—because they're so thin these can burn quickly, so it's important to pay attention. Let cool completely on a rack before serving.

FOCACCIA WITH ROSEMARY

I have a deep affection for fleeting things—summer, my birthday, fresh apricots in July—things that make me happy but vanish seemingly as quickly as they arrive. Focaccia is one of these things. Either it's gone in a flash because it's so good or because simply, like most homemade breads, it's best when fresh and should be eaten just out of the oven. Made very similarly to a pizza crust, with dimpling on the surface and folds on the first rise, this easy bread turns spongier and moister than a crust, courtesy of the additional olive oil and the lift of a second rise. Piney rosemary and lots of flakey sea salt give this snack a potent flavor, one that you can push even further if you like by inserting thin slivers of garlic into the crust before baking. Plan to make this bread as close as possible to when you want to eat it, and then plan to snag some for yourself before you put it on the table. Otherwise you might miss out.

390 grams bread flour (about 2¾ cups)
¼ ounce active dry yeast (about 2½ teaspoons)
2 teaspoons sea salt
¼ cup plus 7 to 8 tablespoons extra virgin olive oil
1 cup warm water
Leaves from 2 to 3 sprigs fresh rosemary
Flake sea salt

Put the flour, yeast, and salt in a food processor and turn the machine on. Add ¼ cup plus 2 tablespoons of the oil through the feed tube first, then add the water in a slow, steady stream. Continue to process for about 3 minutes (the dough should form a ball and ride around in the processor). When the dough is done, it should be shiny, a bit yellow in color (from the oil), soft, and elastic.

Lay a piece of plastic wrap about 12 inches long on a clean work surface. Use your hands to press the dough on the plastic wrap into an 8 x 6-inch rectangle. Press your fingers into the top of the dough all over it, making indentations. With the long side facing you, fold the left third of the dough over and repeat the finger indentions on this folded section. Fold the right third over (as you would a letter) and use your fingers to make the indentations again. Cover the folded dough with plastic wrap and let rise for 30 minutes.

Meanwhile, brush a rimmed baking sheet generously with 1 tablespoon of the oil. When the dough has risen for 30 minutes and is slightly puffed, transfer it to the prepared baking sheet. Gently stretch the dough into a rough 8 x 12-inch rectangle. Once the dough is laid out, brush it generously with 2 tablespoons of the oil, spread the rosemary leaves over the top, and use your fingertips to press holes randomly into the surface of the dough (if the rosemary gets pressed into the dough, that's great too). Be sure to press hard enough to get deep indentations all over the surface.

Cover the dough with plastic wrap and let rise until nicely puffed, another 30 to 40 minutes.

Meanwhile, preheat the oven to 400°F.

Transfer the baking sheet to the oven and bake until nicely golden brown all over, 12 to 15 minutes. Remove from the oven and drizzle immediately with the remaining 2 to 3 tablespoons oil and sprinkle with flake sea salt.

Piney rosemary and lots of flakey sea salt give this snack a potent flavor, one that you can push even further if you like by inserting thin slivers of garlic into the crust before baking.

SALAD THOUGHTS

Growing up we had a salad every night. I can probably count on one hand the number of times there wasn't a bowl of something green and leafy waiting to be passed around table. We ate our salad after dinner—the European way, according to my dad, who had lived in Italy; it was the punctuation mark to every meal, a crisp, fresh ending to whatever more hearty fare had come before. Most nights our salads consisted of lettuce, tomatoes, cucumbers, scallions, and maybe some celery or carrots. But sometimes my mom would add chickpeas or marinated artichokes (an expensive treat), a couple of quartered hearts cut up for the four of us to share. On those nights I would discreetly eat around the creamy beans or tangy hearts, saving them for last, coveting those precious additions for that final bite.

Packaged dressings were forbidden in our house, which is why for a period in my teenage years, as an avid babysitter who spent most weekend nights in the homes of neighbors with less high-minded eating habits than my family's, I regularly looked forward to a solo dinner of iceberg lettuce doused with Seven Seas Italian Dressing. Something about that highly seasoned artificial dressing on the cold, crisp lettuce was just intoxicating to me—a complete contrast to the salads we'd have at home.

My mom's idea of dressing was olive oil and vinegar drizzled straight from their respective bottles, everything then sprinkled with salt and pepper. To this day that is how a salad is dressed in my mother's kitchen, but with a bounty of fresh limes, lemons, and sour oranges in her garden, she's swapped that bottle of vinegar for a squeeze of something citrusy and bracing. And while I'd love to say that I'm different, that I always keep a bottle of homemade, perfectly emulsified vinaigrette in my fridge, that would be a bold-faced lie. I do love a properly made vinaigrette, one with mustard and shallots, maybe some fresh tarragon or dill, but having said that, 90 percent of the time I too just reach for the olive oil and some sherry vinegar (my favorite) and give everything a nice drizzle. It's lazy, but it's light and fresh tasting and doesn't overwhelm the greens or weigh them down. It's also delicious, as my dad will attest. He always used to be the last to reach for the salad bowl, finishing off the last serving, the greens that had sat the longest, nearly marinating in the dressing. To this day I recall goodnight kisses from my father perfumed with my mom's simple vinaigrette. I may have coveted the chickpeas and artichokes, but he was all about the dressing.

Ken and I still eat a salad with dinner pretty much every night. Sometimes it's a more thoughtful creation like the ones here, and sometimes it's simply a dish of sliced tomatoes topped with some basil leaves or dill fronds drizzled with olive oil. Sometimes it's just a bowl of arugula or watercress with a squeeze of lemon, nothing more. Often we fill our dark wooden bowl with a smattering of whatever we have in the house—a bit of this and a bit of that. But we do have some favorite combinations that seem to make a weeknight pizza dinner slightly more special, so here they are. Hardly a comprehensive collection, but these are our keepers.

FAVORITE CHOPPED TRI-COLOR SALAD

Serves 2 to 4

*There's a romantic kind of old-fashioned glamour to depart-
ment store restaurants that I love. My mom used to take us
to lunch at the restaurant in Ohrbach's department store in
Los Angeles for special occasions. I always got a lemonade
and the tostada salad, basically a Mexican salad served in
a huge flour tortilla that had been fried into the shape of a
bowl. It was amazing to me—imagine, you could eat the
bowl! Then Ken and I discovered Fred's, the restaurant that
used to be in the basement of Barneys department store in
New York and is now on the top floor. Fred's is a fabulous
place to go on a Saturday afternoon to people watch and have
a bite to eat, and while we don't do it often, when we do, we
share the Mark's Madison Avenue Salad. It's a chopped salad
that seems to have almost everything you could want in it:
finely chopped lettuce, miniature cubes of beets, lentils, tomatoes, white beans, peas, red onions, Italian tuna . . . it's just
a delicious mishmash of good things. We started making this
salad in the summers for dinner. Then we started abridging
it (skipping the tuna, replacing the beets with jarred pepperoncini and so on) to have with a pizza. It's more than just a
green salad, but not so much work that it can't be pulled
together in less than 10 or 15 minutes. If you have an extra
roasted beet, some leftover peas or corn, or anything else in
the fridge, feel free to throw them in, too.*

¼ cup extra virgin olive oil
2 tablespoons sherry vinegar
1 tablespoon fresh lemon juice (optional)
Sea salt and freshly ground pepper
1 head radicchio, cut into very thin ribbons
1 head endive, cut into very thin ribbons
1 small head romaine lettuce, cut into very thin ribbons
1 cup canned chickpeas or cannellini beans, drained and rinsed
1 cup quartered cherry or grape tomatoes (yellow and red)
¼ cup finely chopped red onion (or to taste)
6 pepperoncini, sliced into thin rings, or to taste
A chunk of Parmesan cheese

In a small lidded jar or bottle, combine the oil, vinegar, and the lemon juice (or omit the lemon juice and increase the vinegar to 3 tablespoons). Season with salt and pepper. Seal and shake well to emulsify. Taste and adjust the oil, acid, or salt and pepper to suit your palate.

In a large bowl, combine the radicchio, endive, romaine, beans, tomatoes, onion, and pepperoncini. Drizzle the dressing over the salad, toss, and adjust seasonings. Use a vegetable peeler to slice wide curls of Parmesan into the salad before serving.

FRUIT, NUT, AND CHEESE SALAD, AS YOU LIKE IT

Serves 2 to 4

This is a salad that you see some version of on many a restaurant menu, and with good reason. It's a tremendous mix of textures and flavors, and you can pretty much make it with whatever you have in the pantry. Ken's favorite combination is tart apples with walnuts and Parmesan. I'm partial to pears or figs with Stilton and pecans in the winter, and nectarines with pistachios and goat cheese in the summer. See? It's not a single recipe so much as a guideline for cobbling something wonderful together, almost effortlessly.

About 4 cups any tender lettuce: mâche, baby arugula, or a combination
½ firm apple or pear or 1 stone fruit of your choice, thinly sliced, or 4 fresh figs, quartered
½ cup toasted pecans, walnuts, pistachios, or hazelnuts
Extra virgin olive oil, for drizzling
Sherry, white, or red wine vinegar, as needed
Sea salt and freshly ground pepper
A crumble or good shaving of goat cheese, Stilton, feta, Parmesan, or any cheese you desire

In a large bowl, combine the lettuce, fruit, and nuts. Drizzle with enough oil to lightly coat everything, followed by a couple tablespoons of the vinegar of your choice. Sprinkle with some salt and a good grind of pepper, toss again, and add the cheese. That's it.

MIDWINTER SALAD WITH BLOOD ORANGES AND POMEGRANATE SEEDS

Serves 2 to 4

I have a few kitchen chores that I absolutely love because they're incredibly calming. Stirring risotto is one and shelling peas another. But one of my favorite tasks is to supreme citrus fruit. To supreme an orange or other citrus means you cut the segments out and separate them from their membranes completely. It's the nicest way to serve pieces of citrus in salad or dessert, and it's really enjoyable to do. First, cut the top and bottom off the orange so you have flat bases. Then cut the peel off the sides by running a knife down from top to bottom, following the curve of the fruit. When you have a nearly naked orange, take your paring knife and cut along the wall of a segment right where the flesh meets the membrane on both sides—a perfect wedge of orange will then be freed from its casing and tumble into a bowl, along with a good bit of juice (save this for the dressing). To make it easier, work every other segment until you've gone around the entire globe, and then do the rest—this helps you maintain some structure. It will take a couple of tries to get it down, but it's oddly rewarding work. This salad will of course work with any sweet citrus, but I'm partial to blood oranges, with their crimson flesh and exotic pebbled skin. Sprinkled with ruby-toned pomegranate seeds, this salad is as striking as it is delicious.

1 small shallot, finely chopped
¼ cup extra virgin olive oil
3 tablespoons fresh blood orange juice (save from supreming)
1 tablespoon Dijon mustard
Sea salt and freshly ground pepper
A good handful of haricots verts (French green beans) or thin string beans, trimmed
About 4 cups mache, baby arugula, or mixed baby lettuces
2 small blood oranges, supremed (see left)
¼ cup pomegranate seeds

In a small lidded jar or bottle, combine the shallot, oil, blood orange juice, and mustard. Season with salt and pepper. Seal and shake well to emulsify.

Bring a medium saucepan of salted water to a boil. Add the beans and cook until they just turn bright green and the water returns to a boil, no more than 3 minutes. Drain, run them under cold water to stop the cooking process, and cut into 1-inch pieces.

In a large bowl, combine the greens, beans, and blood orange segments. Drizzle with the dressing and toss to coat everything evenly. To serve, sprinkle the salad with the pomegranate seeds.

CHEZ GEORGES'S SALADE LYONNAISE

Serves 4

Growing up, my favorite breakfast was poached eggs on buttery toast. My mom had this nifty pan designed to hold little cups suspended above boiling water; it transformed eggs into perfectly shaped domes in mere minutes. So imagine my surprise when I began eating poached eggs elsewhere. At my first New York diner, I was presented with two eggs bobbing, raw and gelatinous, in a puddle of lukewarm water. Another time, at a fashionable brunch spot, I was served eggs as firm as those decorated for Easter. These experiences convinced me of two things: My mom's pan was a very effective modern convenience intended to replace a more traditional technique I wasn't aware of, and most people who were aware of this more traditional technique didn't get it. But a trip to Paris can teach a person many things; for me, it was how to properly poach an egg. Ordering my favorite salad (a salade Lyonnaise) at my favorite brasserie (Chez Georges on rue du Mail), I was faced with an egg slightly ragged around the edges, its wiggly whites blanketing a yolk that spilled out and lay sleepily over the frisée, like a satin coat tossed on a velvet couch. It was a cook's aha moment. Now I'm torn. I love the organic shape and the tender consistency of an egg made the traditional way, but there's something equally perfect about those little white domes. Served on a bed of tangled frisée, dressed in a warm pancetta-infused vinaigrette—both will do the trick alongside a really great pizza.

4 cups torn frisée
$\frac{1}{4}$ cup extra virgin olive oil
4 ounces pancetta, cut into $\frac{1}{4}$-inch cubes
1 small shallot, finely chopped
3 tablespoons sherry vinegar, plus $\frac{1}{2}$ teaspoon for poaching
1 tablespoon Dijon mustard
Salt and freshly ground pepper
4 eggs
$\frac{1}{4}$ cup crumbled Roquefort, Stilton, or other good blue cheese

Put the frisée in a large salad bowl and set aside.

In a medium skillet, heat the oil over medium heat. When the oil is hot, add the pancetta and cook slowly until it's crisp all over, 10 minutes or more. Add the shallot and cook until softened, another minute or two. Add the 3 tablespoons vinegar and the mustard and bring just to a boil, stirring. Remove from the heat.

Meanwhile, set a medium saucepan of water over medium-high heat and add the ½ teaspoon vinegar. Once the water reaches a boil, reduce the heat so it barely holds a simmer and just bubbles gently. Break one of the eggs into a small bowl, being careful not to break the yolk, and slip it into the water, then do the same with the other eggs. Cook the eggs just until the white is set and the yolk has filmed over, 3 to 5 minutes depending on how solid you like your poached egg. Remove each egg with a slotted spoon and allow the water to drain off for a couple of seconds.

If necessary, gently reheat the dressing, then pour it over the greens, add the blue cheese, toss, and season to taste with salt and pepper. Top each portion with an egg and serve immediately.

A trip to Paris can teach a person many things; for me, it was how to properly poach an egg.

ENDIVE, CELERY, APPLE, AND FENNEL SLAW

Serves 2 to 4

There's something about a white salad that's surprising and refreshing, both to eat and to look at on the plate. One of the first I ever tasted was made by Mark Bittman; he shaved raw artichokes, which we both adore, using a mandoline and then paired them with Parmesan and a lemon–olive oil dressing (a version of which is included here on page 200). Nothing more. I was taken by the idea of other similar such salads—hues of crunchy cream and white vegetables tangled up on a plate. I started adding thinly sliced celery to the artichokes, for a barely-there hint of green. Then artichoke season was over and I had to find other vegetables to fill their slot. Endive, apples, and fennel all seemed to make sense. I make this salad mostly in the fall, when the fennel and apples are abundant. But I've also found myself without apples or fennel and used chopped cauliflower instead—it's a different texture completely, but when it's chopped very finely or shaved, it offers up a delightful crunch in contrast to the tender endive. Finished with nutty curls of Parmesan, this white salad complements a pizza perfectly.

1 small shallot, finely chopped
¼ cup extra virgin olive oil
3 tablespoons fresh lemon juice
1 tablespoon Dijon mustard
Sea salt and freshly ground pepper
1 head endive, very thinly sliced into ribbons
2 stalks celery, thinly sliced on an angle
½ bulb fennel, trimmed and very thinly sliced, fronds reserved
½ Granny Smith or other firm, tart apple, very thinly sliced
A chunk of Parmesan cheese (optional)

In a small lidded jar or bottle, combine the shallot, oil, lemon juice, and mustard. Season with salt and pepper. Seal and shake well to emulsify. Taste and adjust the oil, acid, or salt and pepper.

In a large bowl, combine the endive, celery, fennel, and apple. Drizzle with a bit of the dressing, toss to coat, and taste. Add more dressing if needed. To serve, shave wide curls of Parmesan over the salad if desired and garnish with fennel fronds.

SHAVED ARTICHOKE, CELERY, AND PRESERVED LEMON SALAD

Serves 2 to 4

Eating artichokes when I was a kid was a treat. Even though we lived in the state that grew the majority (maybe the entirety) of them, they were still decadent, and two were shared among the four of us. When the season came around and artichokes were both plump and affordable, my mom would use her mother's old pot, line it with a steaming basket, and set the artichokes over a couple inches of boiling water for about 45 minutes. She'd melt butter, add copious amounts of fresh lemon juice, and the four of us would take turns tearing off leaves and dipping them into the silky-sour combination, working our way from the tougher outer leaves inward to the thinner, more creamy-colored tender ones. It always seemed like there was enough to go around until we got to the heart—half a heart was never enough for me. It was a long time before I was introduced to the notion of eating artichokes raw, but as an equal opportunity artichoke lover, it was a fabulous discovery. Baby artichokes are definitely easier to use raw, as you don't have to navigate the choke, but if you're not easily deterred, large ones are fine too. As salads go, this one is a bit more rustic than some, with the thinly sliced vegetables dressed only in olive oil and a few tablespoons of roughly chopped preserved lemons. The flavors are reminiscent of the way my mom used to serve artichokes— the olive oil and the preserved lemons playing the part of the butter-lemon mixture to the artichokes and celery.

1 lemon
8 baby artichokes, bottoms trimmed and tough
    outer leaves discarded
4 stalks celery, very thinly sliced on an angle
Extra virgin olive oil, for drizzling
¼ cup chopped Preserved Lemons (page 30)
Sea salt and freshly ground pepper

Squeeze the juice from the lemon into a large bowl of cold water. Using a very sharp knife, slice the artichokes from top to bottom, as thinly as you can, transferring each slice immediately to the acidulated water to keep them from turning brown.

Place the celery in a large salad bowl. Drain the artichokes of all excess water and add them to the celery. Drizzle the vegetables with enough olive oil to lightly coat everything and toss. Add the preserved lemons, toss again, and season with salt and pepper.

BUTTER LETTUCE AND CHICKPEAS WITH CUCUMBERS AND CRISPY SHALLOTS

Remember those containers of crispy fried onions that used to adorn salads way back when? Yes, they were terrible, awful, so dreadful in fact that as a kid I couldn't get enough of them—the oily residue from the crispy coating leaving my palm shiny and slick as I covertly snacked while ostensibly sprinkling them on the salad. And while thankfully those days are long gone, my affection for crispy onions is not. When I'm nostalgic for them, these more nuanced (and much more delicious) lightly fried shallots do the trick. Combined with velvety lettuce, creamy chickpeas, and a crisp Persian cucumber, the shallots make this relatively straightforward salad both surprising and sassy.

¼ cup extra virgin olive oil, plus more for drizzling
¼ cup cornstarch
3 shallots, thinly sliced into rings
Sea salt and freshly ground pepper
1 head butter, Bibb, or Boston lettuce, torn or cut into ribbons
1 Persian (mini) cucumber, thinly sliced
1 cup canned chickpeas, drained and rinsed
1 to 2 tablespoons sherry vinegar

In a medium saucepan, heat the oil over medium-high heat. While the oil heats, put the cornstarch in a small bowl and add the shallots. Dredge the shallots evenly in the cornstarch, shaking off any excess. When the oil is hot, add the shallots to the pan and cook, turning frequently, until golden brown and crisp all over, about 5 minutes. Use a slotted spoon to remove the shallots from the oil and drain on paper towels. Season with salt and pepper.

In a large bowl, combine the lettuce, cucumber, and chickpeas in a large bowl. Drizzle with enough oil to lightly coat everything and enough sherry vinegar to suit your taste. Toss and taste for seasoning.

To serve, sprinkle the crispy shallots on top of the salad.

ARUGULA, POTATOES, SMASHED OLIVES, AND SOPPRESSATA

Serves 4 to 6

It's apparent at this point how I feel about leftovers for pizza, so it probably doesn't bear saying that I also love to use them in salads. Potatoes, rice, grains, roasted vegetables (asparagus is a favorite), whatever bits and pieces find their way into little bowls or containers in the fridge and need using up. This salad came about because I needed something a littler heartier to go with a vegetable pizza and didn't want to have to run to the store. Finding myself with leftover potatoes from a weekend roast and a hunk of sweet soppressata that was almost too small to notice, I decided to make a collage. The general idea is Provençal in terms of flavor, but it's really just a bunch of odds and ends that comes together nicely.

Sea salt and freshly ground pepper
4 small Red Bliss potatoes, cut into ½-inch pieces
6 cups baby arugula
1 cup cherry tomatoes, halved
½ cup Niçoise or Kalamata olives, pitted
¼ cup cubed thick-cut sweet soppressata, cut into ¼-inch pieces (if thin-cut, ribbons)
2 tablespoons capers, drained
¼ cup extra virgin olive oil
3 tablespoons fresh lemon juice
1 tablespoon whole-grain mustard

Bring a large pot of salted water to a boil. Add the potatoes and cook until a sharp knife just pierces them all the way through, about 8 minutes. Drain.

Meanwhile, in a large bowl, toss the arugula with the tomatoes. On a work surface, use the side of a chef's knife to gently smash the olives, then add them to the bowl along with the soppressata and capers.

In a small lidded jar or bottle, combine the oil, lemon juice, and mustard. Season with salt and pepper. Seal and and shake well to emulsify. Adjust the dressing for seasoning if it needs it.

Add the potatoes to the large bowl (it's good if they're still a bit warm, as the dressing will seep into them nicely and they will wilt the arugula) and drizzle with the dressing. Toss well and serve.

WARM HARICOTS VERTS AND POTATO SALAD WITH PARSLEY

Serves 4 to 6

So why would one serve a potato salad with pizza? One probably wouldn't. But, if one were to decide to make a Butterflied Chicken on the Grill (page 214) for pizza toppings and then realized it looked so good that one just wanted to eat chicken for dinner, and one's crusts were still in the fridge anyway and could wait until tomorrow, then one would need something to serve as both a starch and a vegetable so one didn't have to do anything else except open a bottle of wine. If that hypothetical culinary event were to take place, then one would be in desperate need of a potato-bean salad recipe. And this would be the potato-bean salad that one was seeking. Or if one just really likes potato-bean salad and doesn't see an issue with eating it with pizza, well, then one would still be in great shape.

Sea salt and freshly ground pepper
2 pounds Red Bliss or other creamy potatoes, cut into ½-inch pieces
A good handful of haricots verts (French green beans), trimmed and cut into 1-inch pieces
A good handful of fresh flat-leaf parsley, finely chopped
1 tablespoon whole-grain mustard
2 to 3 tablespoons capers, drained
Extra virgin olive oil, for drizzling
1 lemon, halved

Bring a large pot of salted water to a boil. Add the potatoes and cook until just tender all the way through when pierced with a paring knife, about 8 minutes. Use a slotted spoon to transfer the potatoes to a large serving bowl.

Bring the water back to a boil and add the beans. Cook until just bright green, not much more than a minute or so. Drain and add the beans to the potatoes.

Add the parsley, mustard, and capers to the bowl. Drizzle with enough oil to lightly coat everything, squeeze the lemon into the mix, and toss gently, being careful not to mash up the potatoes too much. Season with salt and pepper and serve warm or at room temperature.

SANS EGG CAESAR SALAD

Serves 2 to 4

If you asked him, Ken would say he doesn't eat anchovies. And I promise you he won't eat a raw egg. It would seem that those two limitations would make Caesar salad a lost cause in our house. Except that when I mash anchovies up with lots of lemon juice and garlic, their strong, salty flavor is subdued. And he's okay with it. I do love the idea of a farm-fresh raw egg to help soften and round out the garlic-anchovy flavor even more, but I'm willing to compromise on that one (unless I've met the chicken, raw eggs scare me just a bit, too). So we make this mock Caesar without the egg but without sacrificing the anchovy. Homemade croutons and a lot of freshly shaved Parmesan make it the perfect match for many a pizza.

3 cups cubed rustic bread
¼ cup plus 2 tablespoons extra virgin olive oil
Salt and freshly ground pepper
2 anchovy fillets (or to taste)
3 tablespoons fresh lemon juice
2 garlic cloves, peeled and smashed
2 small heads romaine lettuce, cut crosswise on an angle into 1-inch ribbons (about 4 cups)
A chunk of Parmesan cheese

Preheat the oven to 400°F.

Place the bread cubes on a rimmed baking sheet and drizzle with 2 tablespoons of the oil. Sprinkle with salt and pepper and toss to coat everything well. Bake until browned, 8 to 12 minutes, turning the cubes at least once so they brown evenly on all sides. Set aside to cool.

Put the anchovies on a cutting board and chop them. Then use the side of your knife to mash them even more, until it's nearly a paste. Transfer the anchovies to a small lidded jar and add the remaining ¼ cup oil, the lemon juice, and one of the garlic cloves. Season with salt and pepper. Seal and shake well.

Rub the remaining garlic clove all over the inside of a large wooden bowl and then discard the clove. Add the lettuce to the bowl and dress with the vinaigrette. Add the croutons and use a vegetable peeler to shave large curls of Parmesan into the salad. Toss again and sprinkle with more pepper.

DANDELION WITH PRESERVED LEMONS AND GARLICKY CROUTONS

Serves 2 to 4

The thing about making preserved lemons is that even though they are preserved, they still won't last indefinitely in the fridge. So when you have a jar, you want to use them. This salad is a simple way to brighten up a pizza dinner and put your preserved lemons to good use—it's both bitter, sour, sweet, and garlicky all at once, and while there aren't many ingredients, there are a lot of textures and flavors bouncing off of each other. If you don't like bitter greens like dandelion, you can certainly swap in something else (romaine would work well in terms of texture); and these croutons, which are one of my old standbys, will make any salad feel a bit heartier. I love the way the lemons seep into the croutons and soften them in spots, so you get both a bit of chew and a bit of crunch.

½ loaf rustic bread, cut or torn into 1-inch cubes
2 tablespoons extra virgin olive oil, plus more for drizzling
3 to 4 garlic cloves, chopped
Leaves from a few sprigs fresh oregano or thyme, chopped
Sea salt and freshly ground pepper
1 bunch dandelion leaves, cut into ribbons
¼ cup Preserved Lemons (page 30), plus some of the juices
Freshly shaved Parmesan, optional

Preheat the oven to 400°F.

On a baking sheet, toss the bread with the oil to barely coat the bread. Add the garlic and oregano or thyme, season with salt and pepper, and toss well to combine. Bake until golden and crisp, 8 to 10 minutes, turning occasionally to make sure the croutons brown on all sides. Remove from the oven.

In a large bowl (I have a big wooden one I like to use), combine the dandelion ribbons, lemons, and some of the juices from the lemons and drizzle with enough oil to lightly coat everything. Toss well. Add some or all of the croutons to the bowl, toss again, taste, and season with salt and pepper if needed. Serve topped with the Parmesan, if desired.

MASTER RECIPES *and* MORE

Most of the recipes in this book for pizza (and everything else really) are short and sweet. But a few depend on the enthusiasm of a cook to do some (relatively) serious cooking, meaning recipes that take some time and energy. Not a ton, but enough that it felt unfair to include them as *part* of the pizza recipe itself without irritating people who just want to make dinner fast. So this chapter is where those longer, slightly more intensive recipes live, along with a couple of stragglers that aren't strictly pizza related, but that are mentioned in the book and might bug people if they were nowhere to be found.

PORCHETTA-STYLE PULLED PORK

I've had porchetta made from a whole pig roasted on a spit in a small Italian town on market day; it was delicious. I've also had a porchetta sandwich at Di Palo's on Mott Street in the rain; it was also delicious. Recently for work I made a pork belly (dried, brined, rubbed, tied, and roasted over 3 days) for a chef's interpretation of porchetta, and it was delicious, too. All of these were authentic and fantastic, but all were all labor intensive beyond words. I wanted to find a way to capture that beautiful garlic-fennel-rosemary-pepper-pork flavor on a pizza without spending 3 days cooking. I suspected that a pork butt would be the ideal cut of meat (read: tasty and affordable) to infuse with a deeply aromatic spice rub if I slow-roasted it in a low oven. My suspicions bore out; in a mere 3 hours I had an abridged version of porchetta ready and waiting to be scattered on a crust. For more intense flavor, rub the pork the night before you plan to cook and let it marinate in the fridge.

3 tablespoons fennel seeds
1 tablespoon juniper berries (optional)
1 tablespoon whole black peppercorns
2 tablespoons extra virgin olive oil
6 garlic cloves, finely chopped
Leaves from 3 to 4 sprigs fresh rosemary
1 tablespoon sea salt
3½ to 4 pounds boneless pork butt
   (pork shoulder), at room temperature

Preheat the oven to 325°F.

In a small skillet, combine the fennel seeds, juniper berries (if using), and peppercorns and toast over medium heat until fragrant, 2 to 3 minutes, tossing frequently. Remove from the heat and either grind in a spice grinder or coffee grinder, or coarsely crush in an old-fashioned mortar and pestle (this is how I do it).

Roughly chop the rosemary leaves. In a small bowl, combine the crushed toasted spices with the oil, garlic, rosemary, and salt and mix well.

Pat the pork dry with paper towels and place it in a roasting pan (with or without a rack—it doesn't really matter, but I don't bother). Rub the pork all over with the spice rub, being sure to get the rub into all the little crevices. Transfer the pork to the oven and roast until the pork can be easily "pulled" with a fork, 3 to 3½ hours. Check the pork every hour or so and baste it with any fat in the bottom of the pan.

When the pork is cool enough to handle, shred it with a fork (or your hands if it's really cooled off). Set aside a cup or so of the meat for the pizza and portion off the rest to freeze for future pizzas—or enjoy as you desire.

SLOW-COOKED SWEET-AND-SPICY PORK

I've mentioned that my beloved husband is a creature of habit. One of his favorite Ken-isms is, "If it ain't broke. . . ." He knows it drives me bonkers, so he says it, looks up grinning like a madman, and lets the words trail off, leaving the platitude unfinished but the thought hanging in the air between us. Things that he likes, well, he likes them to stay the same. Which is why nearly every weekend in the summer, we are required to eat slow-cooked pork of some nature (ribs, butt, or otherwise), with fresh corn on the cob, Cheddar-buttermilk biscuits, and a tomato-something salad. This would be harder for me, someone who craves variation, except that come the dog days, I am a firm believer in keeping cooking simple. Besides the biscuits, the rest of this meal is an entirely outdoor affair that he's happy to manage (we use our outdoor pizza oven for the pork, though an indoor oven at 325°F works just as well). He relishes firing up the pizza oven; he's fine shucking corn on the patio; and he seems to love choosing between the boxwood basil and the scraggly tarragon, when making the salad. He even makes the signature spice rub—a concoction of brown sugar, husky cumin, smoky paprika, and fiery chili that cooks into every crevice of the succulent meat, caramelizing it with the flavor of molasses and warm spices. I suppose, in terms of marital complaints, having a husband who cooks a meal this good (regardless of the frequency) really isn't so bad. I should probably just be quiet and eat.

2 tablespoons smoked paprika
2 tablespoons packed brown sugar, preferably dark
2 tablespoons sea salt
1 tablespoon ground cumin
1 tablespoon chili powder
1 tablespoon freshly ground black pepper
A pinch of red pepper flakes
3½ to 4 pounds boneless pork butt (pork shoulder),
    at room temperature

Preheat the oven to 325°F.

In a small bowl, combine the paprika, brown sugar, salt, cumin, chili powder, black pepper, and pepper flakes.

Pat the pork dry with paper towels and place it in a roasting pan (with or without a rack). Rub the pork all over with the spice rub, getting it into all the little crevices. (If you have leftover rub, it will hold in an airtight container and is delicious as a simple way to perk up pork chops as well.) Transfer the pork to the oven and roast until pork can be easily "pulled" with a fork, 3 to 3½ hours. Check the pork every hour or so and baste it with any fat in the bottom of the pan.

When the pork is cool enough to handle, shred it with a fork (or your hands if it's really cooled off). Set aside a cup or so of the meat for pizza and portion off the rest to freeze for future pizzas—or enjoy as you desire.

WHOLE ROASTED CHICKEN

To me, few things in life exude home and comfort as well as a good roast chicken. There's something hugely satisfying about pulling a glistening, golden brown bird from the oven and watching the fat shimmer on the skin. And the aroma . . . if they could bottle it, it would be called "what home should smell like on a chilly evening." For some reason, though, many really good home cooks are intimidated by the notion of a whole bird. The truth is that a whole chicken is probably one of the simplest, most foolproof dinners you can make. Buy a good-quality bird (ideally it should be free-range and organic, but I admit that's not always possible), rub it with olive oil, season it well with salt and pepper, and roast it for an hour (more or less depending on weight) at 400°F. That's it. Or stuff some fresh tarragon into the cavity and under the skin. Rosemary, thyme, and oregano all work, too. Or slice an onion to throw in the pan. Or . . . well, the options really are limitless. Then either serve it for dinner and use the leftovers for a pizza the next night, or tear it apart and fill your freezer with small portions of lovely roast chicken for future pizzas, pastas, salads, and what-have-you.

1 whole chicken (4 to 5 pounds)
About ¼ cup extra virgin olive oil
Sea salt and freshly ground pepper

Preheat the oven to 400°F.

Wash and dry the chicken well (be sure to pull the neck and giblets out first if it has them). Place the chicken in a roasting pan or large cast iron skillet and rub it all over with the oil. Sprinkle well with salt and pepper. Roast until the juices run clear when pierced with a knife, about 1 hour. Check the chicken every 20 minutes or so to make sure it's not browning too fast. If it is, you can lay a piece of foil over the breast to prevent it from drying out. When the chicken is fully cooked and golden brown, remove it from the oven and let it rest.

When the chicken is cool enough to handle, cut it up into pieces and shred the meat. I like to take off the legs and wings first, then carve the meat off the breasts—then I go back in and pull off as much remaining meat as I can from the carcass. At this point I divvy up the chicken into small portions, put it in baggies, and freeze it so I have multiple pizza topping options on hand all the time. I figure about ½ cup of shredded chicken per pizza. (Be sure to save the bones and any juice that's gathered on your carving board to make a stock or something equally delicious.)

BUTTERFLIED CHICKEN ON THE GRILL

I've admitted that it took me well into my adult cooking life to discover the brilliance of the whole roasted chicken, so I'm only slightly more embarrassed to admit that it took me longer to discover the perfection of a butterflied bird on the grill. Though in fairness, we didn't have an outdoor grill until a few years ago, so there you have it. Anyway, one of my favorite dinners is Ken's butterflied chicken (also known as spatchcocked chicken in fussier culinary parlance). I usually ask my butcher to butterfly my chicken for me out of laziness, but it's easy to do yourself: Simply use your kitchen shears to cut from the neck up one side of the backbone and then down the other—the goal is to remove the backbone while leaving the rest of the chicken intact. Once the backbone is out, lay your bird flat on a work surface breast-side up. Use both hands to press down and flatten the chicken as best you can. Rubbed with olive oil, seasoned on both sides (when you butterfly the bird, you end up with essentially two sides, the outer skin side and the inside) with salt and pepper and lots of chopped fresh tarragon, it's a wonder. Unlike a roast bird that always gets really crispy only on the outside, a butterflied bird has the advantage of getting crisp on all sides, and as you cook it over low heat, the meat stays wonderfully tender. Now you may question my choice of tarragon instead of rosemary, thyme, or even oregano, but years ago,

while reading Simon Hopkinson's absolutely amazing and appropriately titled Roast Chicken and Other Stories, he referred to tarragon as "chicken's favourite herb." An untested flavor combination for me, I decided to give it a try. Almost as if he were standing next to me in the kitchen saying "Didn't I tell you so?" the chicken was spectacular. So while I love the piney taste of rosemary and the smoky flavor of thyme, there really isn't a better partner than this sweet-bittersweet herb when it comes to chicken, in my humble opinion (and Mr. Hopkinson's). Oh, and this recipe is here because if it's August and you want to make chicken for pizza, this beats turning on the oven for a roast.

1 whole chicken (4 to 5 pounds), butterflied (see above)
About ¼ cup extra virgin olive oil
Leaves from 4 to 5 sprigs fresh tarragon, chopped
Sea salt and freshly ground pepper

Wash and dry the chicken well and put it in a large baking dish. Drizzle the bird on both sides with the oil to coat it evenly. Use your hands to coat the bird with the tarragon on both sides and finally sprinkle generously with salt and pepper.

Transfer the chicken to the fridge and let sit, uncovered, for a few hours. (I find keeping it uncovered helps dry out the skin a bit so it will crisp nicely—I know, it's already covered in olive oil so it seems counterintuitive, but it seems to help, so I do it. Call me crazy.)

Remove the bird from the fridge 20 to 30 minutes before you're ready to cook and bring to room temperature.

Preheat the grill to low.

Add the chicken to the grill skin-side up. Cover and grill for about 45 minutes undisturbed or until the skin is nice and crisp all over. Flip the bird and cook for another 10 to 15 minutes skin-side down. Remove from the grill and let rest for a bit before carving.

While I love the piney taste of rosemary and the smoky flavor of thyme, there really isn't a better partner than this sweet-bittersweet herb when it comes to chicken.

KEN'S LIFE-AFFIRMING BOLOGNESE SAUCE

If you've found your way to this recipe, it's likely because you know this is one of my favorites. I'd be torn as to what my last meal on earth would be, but this would certainly make the short list. I've made it before and it's been good. Somehow when Ken makes it, it's otherworldly. As a result, I'm always happy to play sous chef and help chop and taste (usually I taste a bit more often than is truly necessary to the success of the dish), but this is really his domain. Wait for that first winter day when you crave an excuse to stay inside, sit by the fire, and watch the windows fog up from the heat of the kitchen. Start this sauce around noon. Make lunch little more than a light snack and you'll be ready for an early dinner. Pour that first glass of wine just as twilight starts to blanket the sky, make a salad, boil water for pasta, and be sure the seasoning on the sauce is just right. Then enjoy a life-affirming bowl of Bolognese. But don't be greedy. Resist the temptation to have seconds and instead freeze the rest for an easy weeknight dinner. It will be hard to do, but you'll thank me.

2 tablespoons extra virgin olive oil
½ cup chopped pancetta (2 to 3 thick slices)
1 large onion, chopped
2 medium carrots, chopped
2 stalks celery, chopped
Sea salt and freshly ground pepper
½ pound ground pork
½ pound ground veal
½ pound ground beef
½ cup dry white wine
1 can (28 ounces) whole San Marzano tomatoes
1 cup homemade chicken stock
½ cup heavy cream or half-and-half (or more to taste)
Freshly grated Parmesan cheese, for serving

In a large, deep pan, heat the oil over medium-high heat. When the oil is hot, add the pancetta, reduce the heat to medium, and cook until it begins to color on the edges, 6 to 8 minutes. Use a slotted spoon to transfer the pancetta to a small bowl. Reserve the fat in the pan.

Return the pan to medium heat, add the onion, carrots, and celery. Sprinkle with salt and pepper, and cook stirring occasionally, until the vegetables are tender, about 10 minutes.

Return the pancetta to the pan and add the pork, veal, and beef. Sprinkle with salt and pepper and continue cooking over medium heat, stirring to break up any clumps, until the meat is brown throughout, 6 to 8 minutes.

Add the wine to deglaze the pan and cook until it reduces by about half. Add the tomatoes (and their juices) and chicken stock. Reduce the heat to medium-low and use a wooden spoon to gently break up the tomatoes a bit. Continue to cook at a low simmer for about 2 hours, stirring occasionally.

When the mixture is quite thick, add the cream and taste again, adjusting the amount of cream and salt and pepper to suit your taste. Serve over pasta with the Parmesan cheese.

Pour that first glass of wine just as twilight starts to blanket the sky, make a salad, boil water for pasta, and be sure the seasoning on the sauce is just right. Then enjoy a life-affirming bowl of Bolognese.

GARLICKY PASTA WITH CHICKEN, MUSHROOMS, AND WALNUTS

Nothing fancy, just a very comforting bowl of pasta that relies on many of the same ingredients you will probably already have in the house from making pizza. This is one of Ken's favorite dinners and for what it's worth, we've been happily eating it for years. If I don't have leftover chicken and he's craving it, I'll quickly poach a couple of boneless breasts or thighs and then tear those up. Quite rustic, it's the combination of the roasted garlic, ground walnuts, and walnut pieces that give this dish its earthy, decadent spin.

2 tablespoons extra virgin olive oil, plus more as needed
1 cup sliced cremini or button mushrooms
Sea salt and freshly ground pepper
½ cup dry white wine, plus more as needed
½ cup walnuts
2 tablespoons Roasted Garlic Smear (page 29), or more to taste
8 ounces linguine or other pasta
2 cups shredded cooked chicken such as Whole Roasted Chicken (page 213) or Butterflied Chicken on the Grill (page 214)
Leaves from 3 to 4 sprigs of fresh basil, torn or thinly sliced
Freshly grated Parmesan cheese

In a medium saucepan, heat the oil over medium-high heat. When the oil is hot, add the mushrooms, sprinkle with salt and pepper, and reduce the heat to medium. Cook, stirring occasionally, until the mushrooms release their liquid and the liquid evaporates, 10 to 12 minutes. When the mushrooms begin to stick lightly to the bottom of the pan, add the wine and deglaze. Let the mushrooms sauté in the wine until the wine is slightly reduced and the mushrooms are nicely caramelized.

Meanwhile, very finely chop ¼ cup of the walnuts. Add the roasted garlic to the mushrooms along with the chopped walnuts. Stir to combine well and remove from the heat.

Bring a large pot of salted water to a boil for the pasta. Cook the pasta until about a minute from being done. Drain the pasta, retaining about a cup of the cooking water, and set aside.

Toss the chicken with some salt and pepper and add it to the mushroom mixture. If the mixture seems too dry at this point, add a bit more wine and cook over medium heat until the chicken is just warmed through.

Add the pasta to the mushroom and chicken mixture. If the mixture seems dry, add some olive oil or a bit of the reserved pasta cooking liquid to moisten. Break the remaining 1/4 cup walnuts into rough pieces and add to the pan along with the basil. Season with salt and pepper and serve with the Parmesan on top.

Quite rustic, it's the combination of the roasted garlic, ground walnuts, and walnut pieces that give this dish its earthy, decadent spin.

Acknowledgments

I once read somewhere that a book is never written by just one person. In this instance that is certainly true. First, the recipes are inspired by many people—some I know and others I can only dream of meeting, luminous figures I turn to at the stove for guidance, but know only from the tattered and splattered pages of the books they've written that adorn my shelves. Thank you all.

As for the book itself, it too is a collaboration born of the friendship and support of a group of staggeringly wonderful people.

Thank you, Ali Lenzer, my sister, and Jeremy Yun, my brother-in-law, for your sincere and ongoing support in pretty much everything I do, and for helping to give a name to what was, for a time, a nameless book.

Thank you, Andi Delott, for your fierce friendship all these years, honest opinions, and your unrelenting support, no matter what.

Thank you, Jackie McCann. Even from across the Atlantic, you are still the one who can convince me that life is balanced and beautiful when it doesn't feel that way at all.

Thank you, Jen Meyer (and by default her husband, Jeff), my first reader, constant cheerleader, and, lucky for me, someone I can call both friend and family.

continued

continued

Thank you, Evan Sung. You are dear to me on so many levels, and this book might not even be if it weren't for your early contributions.

Thank you, Erica Clark. You touched this book at every stage of the game as listener, reader, cook, and stylist. I'm honored.

Thank you, Elana Hershman, Surfin Percy, Gina Papalia, Dave Sparks, Michaela Hayes, Jenna Helwig, Ashley Schleeper, Katy Andersen, and Kate Schmidt. Each of you cared enough to keep asking, "How's pizza coming?" and then, as true friends do, let me bore you with the details.

Thank you, Al Giangregorio, for being a true-blue pal and building the most glorious pizza oven a girl could ask for.

Thank you, William Brinson, Sam Kaplan, and Quentin Bacon: I've learned a ton from you.

Thank you, Elissa Altman, for recognizing something in my voice and deciding I was worthy of a risk. I am indebted.

Thank you, Dervla Kelly, my unflappable, inspiring editor. You've done nothing but push to make this book more than I thought a book of silly stories and pizza recipes could be. I'm so grateful you inherited me.

Thank you, Kara Plikaitis, for taking this book (and me) in hand and working your butt off to bring this breathtaking volume to life. You are a brilliant art director but also that rare thing: a good friend discovered later in life.

Thank you to everyone at Rodale who touched this book at some point along the way and helped make it better: Jeff Batzli, Mollie Grewe, Nancy Bailey, Kate Slate, and the entire team.

Thank you, Christopher Testani and Carla Gonzalez Hart. I couldn't have asked for a more talented photographer and prop stylist. Your collaborative spirit, creativity, and dedication are beyond words—luckily the images speak for themselves.

Thank you, Angela Miller, my friend and agent, for having the clever idea in the back of a cab that a short little essay about my love for pizza could actually become a book.

Thank you, Mark Bittman, for being such an impossibly supportive human being, for giving me so many mind-boggling opportunities and for teaching me a hell of a lot about food and cooking. You are the bee's knees.

Though it's captured in the dedication, it bears repeating: Thank you, Mom and Dad, for uncensored guidance, unwavering love, and an unsurpassed example of how to live a happy life.

And thank you, Ken. Getting to sit across the table from you at the beginning and end of each day—often over a pizza—makes everything okay.

Index

Boldfaced page references indicate photographs.

About the author

Suzanne Lenzer is a graduate of the Institute of Culinary Education. A successful food stylist and writer, she has worked for many years with *New York Times* columnist and cookbook author Mark Bittman. Her styling has appeared in the *New York Times* magazine, *Food Network* magazine, and *O* the Oprah magazine, among others, as well as in more than a dozen cookbooks. As a writer, Suzanne has had her work appear in the *New York Times,* and she has cowritten several cookbooks. Suzanne lives with her husband in Manhattan and Connecticut. Visit her at www.suzannelenzer.com.